You're All Grown Up, Vancouver!

text by
Margaret Evans

drawings by
Barb Wood

ISBN 0-88839-996-0
Copyright © 1987 Margaret Evans

Canadian Cataloging in Publication Data

Evans, Margaret 1944 -
  You're All Grown Up, Vancouver!
  ISBN 0-88839-996-0

1. Vancouver (B.C.) - History - Juvenile literature. 2. Vancouver (B.C.) Miscellanea.
I. Title.

FC3847.33.E93 1987   j971.11'33   C86-091587-5
F1089.5.V22E93 1987

All rights reserved. No part of this publication may be reproduced, stored in a retrieval system or transmitted, in any form or by any means, electronic, mechanical, photocopying, recording or otherwise, without the prior written permission of Hancock House Publishers.

Edited by Diane Brown
Typeset & Paste-up by Karline Johansen
Design by Herb Bryce
Printed in Canada by Friesen Printers

COVER: Barb Wood drawing of steam clock in Gastown

INSIDE FRONT COVER: Barb Wood drawing of City Hall of 1898-1923

Published simultaneously in Canada and the United States by

HANCOCK HOUSE PUBLISHERS LTD.
19313 Zero Ave., Surrey, B.C. V3S 5J9

HANCOCK HOUSE PUBLISHERS
1431 Harrison Avenue, Blaine, WA 98230

Contents

	Introduction	6
1.	**Infant Days**	8
	Engineer Vancouver's 'Godfather'	9
	The Three Greenhorns	12
	The first train thrills us all	15
	The 'galloping' trolley...	17
	John "Gassy Jack" Deighton	18
2.	**Off to School**	20
	Kids can, too, spell	21
	Rules for Teachers	24
	A lesson in loyalty	24
	When is an island not really an island?	25
	Dress code for students	29
	The case of Billy Butt-insky	29
3.	**Having Fun!**	30
	Crazy George made music	32
	The creek, the fire, the fun!	34
	Bringing music to the city	36
	Vancouver on display: The PNE	38
	The thrill of a night time...	40
	This city has five sisters	44
4.	**Growing Up is Hard to Do**	45
	Vancouver's Stanley Park Zoo	48
	The Vancouver Aquarium	54
	Highlights of 100 years of Policing	56
	The Carey Fir Legend	56
5.	**Protecting Vancouver**	57
	The city's fathers say	58
	Dogs in police work	60
	Vancouver General Hospital...	65
	A Great city	67
	A mammoth tale of dating	70
6.	**For the Sport of it all**	71
	The origins of hockey	74
	The Royal Hudson Number 2860	76
7.	**Vancouver Goes to Work**	77
	A Test of Faith	80
	The symbol of Chinese pigtails	81
	The silk train express...	82
	The cultivation of silk	83
	The Port of Vancouver...	83
	Golden Prairie nugget	91
	Airways not for birds	92
	Vancouver International Airport	94
	The Story of Captain George Vancouver	95
	More books to read	96
	Quiz-z-z-z	96
	Mayors of the City of Vancouver	IBC

A book is not written alone. Many people and institutions helped in the search for the information that tells the story of Vancouver. I would like to thank:

Margaret Weir	Jack Drain
Eleanor Trasolini	Mrs. M. Whitechurch
Harry Bancroft	Kevin Davies
Ruth Phillips	Thomas Balabanov
Janet Vigner	Geraldine Batt
Mary Lade	Jessie Evans
Nora Parker	Eric Grisdale
Mary Rutherford	Valerie Milner

Acknowledgements

I also acknowledge with thanks the help of:

The staff at the Vancouver Centennial Museum
The staff at the City Archives
Vancouver Public Library
Langley Library, "Remember When" Doll Museum
Vancouver General Hospital
Vancouver City Police Department
Vancouver Fire Department
Mining Association of British Columbia
The Council of Forest Industries

Grateful thanks is extended to all those individuals and companies who assisted me in the compilation of this book.

Of special assistance have been the papers of the late Dr. Gladys C. Schwesinger.

This book was published in celebration of Vancouver's Centennial with the financial assistance of the Vancouver Centennial Commission.

Dedication

To Michelle, Kennie, and
Jonathan for memories of growing
up days.

Introduction

This is how Vancouver looked in May, 1886, a month after being incorporated. The maple tree stood on the corner of Carrall and Water Streets. The tree was used as a notice board and as a place for the men of Vancouver to hold meetings!

It is a city that has so much to give to so many different kinds of people. Parks...theatres...shopping malls...wading pools...music...mountains...international business...the herbs of Chinatown...festivals...memories of Gastown...the scent of cedars...the crashing of waves...the lights of Christmas...the polar swim...and lots, lots more.

In 1986, Vancouver celebrated its 100th birthday. As one of Canada's youngest cities, its centennial fell a long way behind the centennials of some eastern cities. When Vancouver was born in 1886, Halifax, on Canada's east coast, had already had one centennial and was celebrating its 137th birthday! In 1886, Toronto was boasting about its opera house, its college, and its brand new provincial Parliament Buildings.

But what was happening in the eastern part of the country in 1886 might just as well have been happening in another world as far as Vancouver was concerned.

Vancouver existed in a wild, lonely part of the country, cut off from the east by formidable mountain ranges and thousands of miles of prairie. In almost every way, young Vancouver was very much alone. It had to survive and grow on the abilities of the people who came here and the local resources they could find.

The birth and growth of a city are like the birth and growth of a child.

First, there are the nursery years—the early years when the city is formed with its own laws and boundaries and the first residents find work and build homes, stores, churches, and schools.

Then come the learning years when the city's activities develop. Its activities are its commerce and industries. The people of the city discover what products they can make and sell to other towns, cities, and countries. They find the most economical way to make these products. They learn the most skilful way to market them.

The learning years are the growing years. A city grows not only by having more and more people coming to live in it but also by developing a variety of industries and businesses. This attracts more and more people with different kinds of skills.

As the city grows up, it earns for itself a reputation among other cities and countries as a supplier of many kinds of goods. Through this foreign trade, the city becomes more and more important.

Today, Vancouver is known all around the world. People come here from all over the world, not only to enjoy a vacation but also to trade and to do business with Vancouver-based industries.

This book is about Vancouver's birth and growth as seen through the eyes of a child. Her name is Mary-Margaret. She isn't a real child. She represents all the children who were born and raised here and who knew what it was like growing up in a city that was also growing up. Mary-Margaret shares her fears and her laughter, her excitements and her disappointments as she remembers Vancouver's growing up days.

Everywhere you looked, people were building houses! These houses were built looking east of Abbott Street 3 weeks before the Great Fire in June, 1886.

Publisher's file

1. Infant Days

It's funny, I can still remember that day in April when Vancouver was born. It was strange, getting used to a new name. I mean, we'd always called our settlement Granville. And here we were with the same town—but a brand new name!

The people were excited though. All the parents kept talking about the railroad that was being built to link us to the east. And about the ships that docked near the mills to be loaded up with spars and masts and lumber. And the new buildings going up and the new stores that were opening and. . . .

Oh! I didn't introduce myself. I'm Mary-Margaret. I grew up as Vancouver was growing up. But, do you know, it very nearly didn't grow up at all!

You see, something really AWFUL happened. It was a Sunday. I remember the date. It was June 13, 1886. My baby brother John's first birthday. To celebrate, Mama and Daddy had taken us to the beach

The fire that destroyed Vancouver was as terrifying as this forest fire!

for a picnic.

Back then, there was still a lot of forest close to the city. Every day, though, people worked at clearing it. They cut the trees and burned the bush and, that Sunday, there were still some bush fires burning not far away.

Because it was such a hot day, Daddy and I went to wade in the tidal pools and search for crabs under the rocks. Just the little ones. The big ones pinch too hard!

Anyway, suddenly, for no reason, a terrific wind blew up. It came right at us across Burrard Inlet. It really howled. How it scared me! It knocked me over. I heard John scream. In the town, I heard a church bell ring.

Suddenly Mama screamed. Not just an angry scream. A real frightened scream. I looked up and FROZE! All I could see was this raging fire roaring through the forest. It was heading straight for town.

"In the water!" Daddy screamed at all of us, "NOW!"

He didn't have to tell me! The fire was getting closer and closer and it felt so hot even the air felt like it was burning. I dived into the waves and Mama tumbled into the water carrying John, who was screaming his head off. So was everyone else who raced for the water or tried to hide in wells or hollows.

Engineer Vancouver's 'Godfather'

Lauchlan Alexander Hamilton is known as the "Godfather of Vancouver."

He was born in eastern Canada in 1852 where he became a civil engineer and began working for the Canadian Pacific Railway. He came to Vancouver in 1883 when he was 31 years old.

Hamilton was the C.P.R.'s first land commissioner. His job was to survey the wild land and lay down and name the first streets.

In the fall of 1885, Hamilton and a party of 8 men began staking out the first 4 streets of Vancouver.

The first street he named was Hastings, after the pathway that led to Hasting's Mill.

The cross-street he named after himself, Hamilton.

He named Abbott Street after a Mr. H. H. Abbott, general superintendent of the C.P.R. in British Columbia. He named Cambie Street after Henry John Cambie, a C.P.R. consulting engineer.

Lauchlan Hamilton was a senior alderman when the terrible fire destroyed Vancouver in June, 1886. It was he who obtained a tent and set up the first city hall in it while the ground was still warm from the flames. It was Hamilton who asked the Dominion government for the military park to be leased to the city as a park for everyone and it was he who designed Vancouver's first coat of arms.

Hamilton died in Toronto in 1941.

The first postal service in British Columbia was run by the offices of the Hudson's Bay Company. Fur traders and travelling company officials would take people's mail with them and leave it at the trading posts for pickup.
Everyone appreciated the service. In a resolution passed by the Legislative Assembly in Victoria in 1857, it was noted, "...that the Assembly acknowledge the Colony to be under great obligations to the Hudson's Bay Company for the kind...manner in which they have carrier... letters..."

The first letter sent in British Columbia was written by explorer David Thompson. He wrote it somewhere on the Columbia River and sent it to the Officer-in-Charge at Fort St. James in 1811. It travelled to its destination by being handed from one Indian band to another until it arrived in Fort St. James 8 months later...

The ferry service from Vancouver to West Vancouver started in 1909 and ended in 1947.

The ferry service from Vancouver to North Vancouver started in 1866 with Navvy Jack's rowboat.

We stayed in the water for an hour and watched, horrified, as the whole town burned! Never, ever, have I been so scared as that day. No one could stop the fire. The flames raced faster than a man could run. I can still remember the sight of one man racing for his life but a flame caught his leg and...I don't think there was anything left of him.

It was SO hot that buildings burst into flames even before the fire reached them. I was watching one that had been newly painted. It sort of shimmered and there were these waves of heat and then...BOOM! It exploded into a white wall of flame.

I saw the roof blow off the soda factory and huge chunks of wood were thrown into the air by the exploding blasts. People were screaming and crying everywhere and I even saw Daddy cry.

When it was all over, we went to find our house. On the way we went by St. James' Church where the bell had been rung. There wasn't any church. And there wasn't any bell anymore either. All that was left was a pool of molten bronze oozing through the black pieces of the steeple. I remember how I shuddered. We'd gone to church in that very church that morning—only a few hours ago.

Our house had perished like the church. It had been burned to the ground. Mama cried so much when she saw the ruins, but Daddy made us realize how lucky we were. We weren't among the 20 people who had died or the many who had been hurt.

"We'll build a new house," he said, "it'll be even better than before."

And that's what we did. There was no time to be sad. The next day was Monday and, everywhere, people were starting to build houses and stores again. There was even a city hall. It was a tent.

And d'you know what the first thing the city

aldermen did? They bought a fire engine and a fire bell. And they passed a law that said that houses had to be built more sturdily. That's why lots of the new buildings were made with brick and stone. Like ours.

How Mama loved it! The parlour was big with a high ceiling and long, narrow windows. It looked out onto a street full of wild pansies, forget-me-nots, and buttercups. The kitchen was panelled with dark brown stained wood and there was brown trim everywhere, making the kitchen always seem dark. There was a huge sink and copper taps and brown shelves and a pantry.

But the best room of all was mine. It was in the attic. It was painted in brown wood trim and it had a tiny window that looked out over the city to the mountains across the Inlet.

Every night I would stare out at the city and count the new buildings. There was always something new—a store, a bank, houses or a school, stables or another saloon. I couldn't wait to try out the new roller-skating rink and Mama never failed to take us to the new church that had been built on the corner.

From my attic window, I could even see the forest of the Military Reserve. But something special happened to change that.

Mama and Daddy. How like so many pioneers they were!

Vancouver's first City Hall was a tent! It was erected right after the Great Fire.

The Three Greenhorns

The settlement of the region that would later be the City of Vancouver was started by 3 Englishmen: John Morton, Samuel Brighouse, and William Hailstone.

One day, in 1862, Morton saw a lump of coal sitting in a store window in New Westminster. He thought that, where there is coal, there must be clay. John Morton was a potter and he thought that, with clay, he could make bricks. With bricks, he could start a business and become wealthy.

With the help of an Indian, he explored the shores of Burrard Inlet where the coal had come from. In October, 1862, he found some good clay.

With his two friends, Samuel Brighouse and William Hailstone, John Morton filed a claim to 223 hectares of land around the site. Today, we recognize that site as downtown Vancouver!

At first, everyone in New Westminster laughed at the 3 men who wanted to make bricks in the wilderness by the inlet. The 3 friends were nicknamed "Three Greenhorns" because they were thought not to know any better.

But the Englishmen had the last laugh. They built a cabin and a small barn, packed in a cooking stove and, in a rough kiln, began to make the first bricks in British Columbia. Ever since, they have been honoured as Vancouver's first settlers.

1) I spy with my little eye
   A terminal near a Big Mac.
   It's the end of the line.
   And it's there that you'll find
   All those things that go
   Clickety-clack!

One of the city aldermen was a man called Mr. Hamilton. He was a friend of Daddy's and he was determined that the reserve was going to be a park for everyone. Daddy thought it was a wonderful idea. Mr. Hamilton and some other aldermen asked the Dominion government if the city could have the use of the reserve as a park for everyone. They told the government officials they would pay a fee every year for the use of it. No one was happier than Daddy and Mr. Hamilton when the government agreed. And no one was more confused than me!

You see, everywhere around us was forest. And there were bears and beavers and raccoons and deer all over the place. Well, sort of. What did we need a park for when we lived in the wilderness anyway?

Daddy told me. He could see the day when all the forest around us would be gone and the city would spread all the way to the banks of the Fraser River. A park would remind people what Vancouver once looked like when it was only forest. I didn't believe him for a second! A city all the way to the river...? NEVER! Now, though, I know what he meant.

Anyway, the city leased the Military Reserve from the Dominion government for one dollar a year. Daddy told me a lease was like a fee you had to pay each year to borrow something.

When it came to naming the park, the city aldermen asked the governor general if they could use his name. He was called Lord Stanley of Preston. He agreed and the Military Reserve got to be called Stanley Park.

Lord Stanley even came out to open the park officially in 1889. What a day! Everyone dressed up and there were streamers and banners and speeches and Lord Stanley dedicated the park, "For the use and enjoyment of peoples of all colours, creeds, and customs for all time. . . ."

I can remember another day of streamers and banners. It was even MORE exciting. It was May 23, 1887, and Mama told me that it was the last day

Clearing. Burning. Building. This was what it was like in Vancouver during its very early years.

Vancouver would ever be separated from the rest of Canada. I'd never thought of it as being separated in the first place but I didn't want to spoil Mama's excitement so I didn't tell her that.

It was the day the first train came to Vancouver. What a sight! Thousands of people dressed up in their best clothes. The Fire Brigade marched to greet it and the band played.

The Engine was No. 374 and it was just COVERED in flowers and streamers. It pulled a baggage car, a sleeper, a first-class car, a Pullman, and a drawing car. Its smokestack had a sign that said MONTREAL GREETS THE TERMINAL CITY and there was a picture of Queen Victoria on its headlight.

Mama and Daddy took us down to greet the train. I even touched the hot, shiny metal side. It had been polished so much you could see yourself in it! There was something exciting about touching it. Like touching the future. The sound of its whistle and the itching smell of the smoke made me suddenly excited about growing up. I promised myself I'd go on a train one day. I would travel and see Canada and the United States and....

I remember while I was making myself all these promises, one of the crew came up to me and gave me a flower from the front of the engine. I was so excited, I forgot how to say "thank you." It was a wild rose from the prairies, he told me. That night, Mama showed me how to press and dry it. I've kept it ever since.

The year of 1887 was one of "firsts." Less than a

Up and down the coast of British Columbia, timber stood tall and proud!

month after the first train arrived, the first passenger steamship from the Orient docked in Vancouver. She was the *Abyssinia* and she was one of 3 Cunard ocean liners that would regularly sail between Japan and Vancouver.

There was something special on board the ship besides the 100 Chinese passengers, letters, newspapers, and other goodies. She was carrying tea and silk. Tonnes of it.

Some of the tea was going to London, England. In the past, tea clippers had sailed as fast as they could from the Orient to England taking shipments of tea. But now that there was an overland railway route across Canada, shippers wondered if they could ship tea faster by sending it overland across Canada than by sea to England.

The tea was taken off the *Abyssinia* and loaded onto a train which raced to Montreal. Then it went by another train to New York where it was loaded on board a steamer which sailed to London.

Baby Billy, Mama, John, and me enjoying a tree in Stanley Park!

The *Abyssinia* had docked in Vancouver on June 14. The tea arrived in England on June 29. The whole journey from Yokohama to London had only taken 29 days. That was 2 weeks faster than the journey taken by the famous tea clippers!

"That'll put Burrard Inlet on the map!" Daddy had boasted. Vancouver wasn't just a place to buy lumber from anymore. Countries could now send their goods here and, because of the railway, we could send them all the way across the nation. Vancouver was getting important!

In the 1890s, it got even MORE important. With all the Oriental, American, and European people coming and going all the time, all kinds of building was going on. There were offices and stores and houses and churches and stables and hotels and carbarns.

Carbarns! Do you know what they were for? Streetcars!

What a sight THEY were! And what a ride! John called them rumble-bumpers because, as they rumbled around corners, you'd bump into other passengers.

I can remember the first day they were in use. It was June 29, 1890. For a treat, Daddy took us on one.

"What's that for?" John asked Daddy, pointing to the wire above.

"That's where the power comes from to make it go," he said.

The first train thrills us all . . .

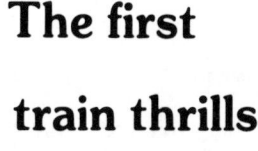

One of the most exciting days in early Vancouver history was the arrival of the first train. Those up the line in the Fraser Valley were the first to cheer it down the track.

Farmers and Indians, merchants, and children all shrieked, "She's Coming! She's COMING!" the moment they heard the first faint distant whistle.

The crowd went wild when they first caught sight of Locomotive 374 with her string of cars behind. Arms, hands, and hats were all waving frantically as the engineer, Peter Righter, opened the cylinder-cocks to let the steam shoot right up to the feet of the crowd. Then he pulled the throttle wide open with one hand as he pulled the whistle down hard with the other. What a shriek the little engine made!

Whistling and clacking the last few miles into Vancouver, the train was greeted by a city of people decked in the brightest of their celebration colours. Houses,

continued on page 16

Looking at the entrance to the new Stanley Park. The shelter on the right was a streetcar waiting room.

Vancouver City Archives.

The first train thrills us all...

continued from page 15

horses, and wagons were alive with coloured streamers. Everyone wore their best clothes. Posters and placards welcomed the train everywhere.

It was 12:45 p.m. when, with every ear in the city straining and every eye turned eastward up the track, the first echo of a whistle was heard.

"Here she comes!" everyone screamed.

A minute later, amid cheers, ringing bells, and the playing of a band, the train hissed to a stop in Vancouver. The roar was deafening, but after it had died down a bit, Mayor MacLean read a welcome to Superintendent Abbott:

"We have assembled here today to welcome the arrival of the first through train, which is the greatest event in the history of our city and which is of the utmost importance to the province at large."

After the speeches, everyone swarmed around the engine, reaching out to stroke the shining brass and steel, gaze with wonder at the wheels that had come so far, and ask question after question.

The engine, a wood-burner, was decorated with flags, evergreens, and shields. Signs commemorated the historic journey and Queen Victoria's picture adorned the front.

As the crew—Righter, the engineer; George Taylor, the fireman; and Peter Barnhart, the conductor—greeted and shook hands with everyone, a little girl shyly asked one of them for a souvenir. She was given a few flowers from the engine's decorations. Clutching her treasure, she later preserved them, and today, those flowers lie in the City Archives as a colourful reminder of a day of excitement in early Vancouver— May 24, 1887.

Engine No. 374 pulling the first train to arrive in Vancouver.

I could barely wait for it to go. The seat was open-ended and I was sitting right at the end by the running board. I couldn't care less how it went, so long as it went. NOW!

"How?" asked John. He could be so demanding sometimes.

"The power comes down the pole and into the bus," Daddy told him, being very patient.

"Why?"

"Daddy just TOLD you that," I said, getting exasperated.

"To make the wheels go round," Daddy said just as the conductor came alongside us on the running board and asked, "Fares please!"

"What's a fare?" asked John.

"It's what you pay to ride the streetcar," I hissed at him.

"Give this to the conductor, Mary-Margaret," said Daddy, handing me 3 nickels. One each.

I was handing the nickels to the conductor when John said in his loudest I-want-to-know voice so all the other passengers could hear, "Do we get the fares back when we get off?"

Was I embarrassed? Everyone laughed, including

The 'galloping' trolley and the defiant little sister!!!

Just as Vancouver's fast moving traffic is a constant danger to children today, so the galloping trolleys of its early years were a hazard to youngsters back then.

And there was always a daring child to defy them.

When Gladys Schwesinger was barely 5 years old, she grew tired of always having to obey her older sister Ellen. One day, as they were about to cross the road, Gladys rebelled and refused her mother's rule of holding Ellen's hand while crossing.

Having broken one rule and challenged Ellen's authority, Gladys broke another rule and stood stock still in the middle of the road.

Ellen started to get panicky.

"Gladys, come ON!" she shouted.

How we loved to ride the modern day streetcars!

"No," Gladys said defiantly. And, just as a trolley came into view at the top of the hill, she sat down on the track.

By now, a number of other children had stopped to watch what was happening. As the trolley rolled nearer and nearer, they, too, pleaded with Gladys to get up and get out of the way.

"No," she said again.

Inside, Gladys was a turmoil of triumph and fear. For the first time, she'd learned that her sister could be defied. But could the rollicking streetcar?

"Come ON!" pleaded one of the children.

"PLEASE!" begged Ellen.

"You're gonna get KILLED!" panicked the boy.

By now, Gladys could feel the vibration of the trolley on the track. With sudden fear—she froze! She couldn't get up. She couldn't even MOVE.

"I...c...can't...." she started to say.

Frantically the children grabbed her and tried to drag her from the track. The trolley was so close now that they could see the driver's terrified face as he tried to slow the speeding car.

"HELP!" screamed the children.

And, in the nick of time, help came. From out of nowhere, a man leaped forward, scooped the terrified, fear-frozen Gladys from the road and rushed to the other side where he tripped and rolled into the bushes with the screaming little girl just as, in a swirl of wind and dust, the trolley thundered by and on down the hill.

Gladys never did remember what her punishment was for defying her sister that day. But she remembers that she learned two things: one was the power of fear; and the other was that a child should not challenge an older sister's authority—she may not be lucky enough to be rescued the next time.

John "Gassy Jack" Deighton

One of the most colourful men in the history of Vancouver was John Deighton. When he arrived, on September 30, 1867, Vancouver was still known as Granville. Mr. Deighton brought with him his wife, a few of her relatives, and a small collection of animals. He also brought a barrel of whiskey.

Because of his whiskey, Mr. Deighton became the most popular man in the settlement. He offered free drinks of whiskey to anyone who would help him build a saloon.

Never in the history of Vancouver have saws, hammers, lumber, and nails appeared so fast! Within 24 hours, Deighton House was built and its doors were open for business.

Speaking from its rooftop, Mr. Deighton unfurled the Union Jack flag, swore his loyalty to it, thanked everyone for their help, then jumped down and began pouring drinks.

John Deighton was a master mariner. He had travelled the world and was very well informed about the events of the times. He was generous, witty, and talkative. It was because he was so talkative that people started called him "Gassy Jack" among themselves.

Of course, they would never call him that to his face. It was just a fond nickname they had for him like many nicknames given early settlers. The nicknames would often reflect the kind of people the settlers were.

There was "Holy Joe," "Sore Neck Billy," "Happy Jack," "Navvy Jack," "Crazy George," "Dutch Pete," "Portugese Joe," "Jericho Charlie," "Howe Sound Jim," "Squamish Jacob," and "Capilano Joe."

Even the name of the settlement—Gastown—was really a nickname taken from Gassy Jack. The official name, then, was Granville.

"Gassy Jack" Deighton giving his speech on the rooftop of his new saloon.

the conductor and they all looked at ME. John slid to the floor and Daddy went all red as he tried to find him.

But we loved the streetcars. As all of us were growing up, Mama used to let us ride the streetcars for the fun of it. My youngest brother, Jimmy, would spend 5¢ riding the streetcar around and around between Granville, Main, Broadway, and Hastings Streets. That circle route was called the Fairview Belt Line. He would ride it ALL day. And for just 5¢!

The 1890s were very exciting years for all the children. Especially 1898. Suddenly, thousands of people were arriving in Vancouver. Neither John nor I could understand why, all of a sudden, everyone wanted to come to Vancouver. Daddy told us about the gold that had been discovered in the tributaries of the Klondike River in the Yukon. Of course, we didn't know where that was except it was somewhere in the far north.

I had never SEEN so many people. Prospectors and

outfitters were outfitting themselves with everything they could find that would help them find gold.

Which was where John helped out.

"What are you doing?" I asked, staring at a pile of wood and nails and 2 stray dogs.

"You'll see," he said in his you'll-see voice, which meant he was up to something.

Well, I did see. In no time, John had made each dog a little wagon and harness. He trained each dog, which he called Huff and Puff, to pull the wagons and he sold the teams to the prospectors. Wow, did John's little enterprise soon catch on with the children in the street! Soon, all of us were teaching dogs to pull wagons and selling them for a profit.

Mama didn't know what to make of it but Daddy just laughed and told her to let us have our fun. It was healthier than running wild in the streets or muddying up the house with dirty boots.

She couldn't really argue that so we carried on dog training. But, by 1900, the goldfields up north were picked bare of the precious mineral and life got back to normal.

See how Engine No. 374 was decorated with flowers?

Provincial Archives, Victoria

The Hastings Sawmill School. This photo was taken in July, 1886.

2. Off to School!

I loved school! Everyone did. You might not think that doing sums on our slates was any better than doing chores. But it was for me. Because I liked sums. I liked printing, too. And geography and history and literature. But my favourite, like everyone's, was music. How we loved to sing! The teachers, too. Why, even in the early 1900s there were singing festivals where our schools used to perform.

The first school in the area was built at Moodyville right by the mill. This area is now North Vancouver. That was in 1870. You see, Mr. Sewell Moody, who built the mill, employed a man called George Washington Haynes. He was the superintendent. Mama told us that he had come to Burrard Inlet from Maine. He went back there in 1869 to marry Miss Adelaide Hart. When he was home, he asked his sister, Laura, to come back with him to Moodyville to teach the children of the men who worked at the mill.

Miss Laura A. Haynes, the first School Teacher on Burrard Inlet. Miss Haynes taught the children of the men who worked at the Moodyville Mill. She arrived at Burrard Inlet in 1869.

Mrs. Duncan Roderick Reid, the first Lady School Trustee in Vancouver.

She really liked that idea, so she did. And that's how she came to be the first teacher in Burrard Inlet. Vancouver wasn't Vancouver then, but known as "Granville." The School Act was passed in 1872, and in that year, a school was built in Granville. Miss Georgina Sweeney was hired as its teacher. She was paid $40 a month. That doesn't seem like much now! But it was then.

Actually, the School Act wasn't very fair to Laura Haynes. One of its rules was that you had to have a teaching certificate to teach. Miss Haynes didn't have one. Even though she had been doing a good job teaching the Moodyville children, she had to leave the school. Mrs. Murrey Thain, who did have a certificate and who was the wife of one of the mill's stevedors, became teacher.

In 1886, the Granville school was destroyed in the Great Fire. But a private school opened at the end of July that year. In the fall, another private school opened. It had moved here from New Westminster. It was called Lorne College and its principal was Mr. Fiennes Clinton, the brother of the Anglican minister.

By 1890 there were 5 schools in Vancouver with 13 teachers and 1,024 students. That was the year the first high school opened. Guess how many students that had ...THIRTY-ONE!

Schools were always painted in dark colours then.

Kids can, too, spell

In 1941, there were complaints among School Board members that children could not spell as well as they used to when the "Three R's" (reading, 'riting, and 'rithmetic) were taught.

Mr. McCorkindall, who was the superintendent of schools, said that was not true. He remembered a story about an Ottawa School Board man who had said the same thing about his own son's spelling abilities. Another man had overheard him and had decided to test what he claimed.

This other man got an old exam paper from the Ottawa school where the man on the School Board had gone and gave the exam to both the man and his son. The results? Father — 60%; Son — 80%!

This proved Mr. McCorkindall's point that the kids of the 1940s were doing just as well, even better, than the kids of the early 1900s...

All the children loved school!

1st typewriter in B.C.

Everything was dark brown. I suppose it didn't show the dirt as much. In fact, ALL buildings were painted in dark colours. Even our kitchen. It had brown-stained woodwork and the lower half of the walls were panelled with brown coloured wainscotting.

I can still remember my earliest days in school. Even the first day. I was so nervous. Mama took me and left me with the teacher. Well, she talked to me for a few minutes then got on with teaching the class.

I felt so embarrassed, standing there with all those children staring at me. I had to stand because there were no empty seats at first and the teacher said she'd find me one during recess. It seemed like FOREVER before recess came!

All the children ran out and I followed them. I'd never felt so alone. Mama had abandoned me, I thought, and I couldn't wait to go home.

Provincial Archives, Victoria

Suzie and me.

2) I spy with my little eye
Creatures that once walked on land.
The weather got cool.
Now they dive in a pool
And one of their pals is a man.

That was when a girl came up to me. I had seen her in the classroom and she had sat at the back, by the window. She had green eyes and long blonde hair and a funny lopsided smile. I still remember it, because it was the first smile I saw in school. And, when she asked me if I wanted to play skip with her, she became my first friend. Suzie has been my best friend for the rest of my life.

School was fun from then on. Except the day I was late. Was I scared! You see, the school had big steps leading up to the huge brown entrance doors that were always open until lessons started. Then they were closed.

Well, I got there when the doors had already closed. There was no way I was going to go up the steps and open them. So I went home. Mama was so cross with me. She sent me to bed for the day for being so naughty.

But, you know, there were days when Mama used to keep me out of school to do chores and help care for my little brothers. Lots of parents did that. I didn't mind helping but Mama always chose a day when we had painting. I loved to paint but Mama always thought it was such a stupid thing and a waste of time. She didn't see any point in sending me to school on painting days. So that was why I stayed home. I remember I once asked

The idea of the need to protect wildlife and enforce conservation laws is nearly as old as Vancouver. In September, 1891, a citizen wrote that he had seen 2 dead does for sale on Cordova Street and that, if there was no Game Protection Society to protect wild animals, the deer would soon be as rare as the buffalo.

RULES FOR TEACHERS 1872

1) Teachers each day will fill lamps, clean chimneys.
2) Each teacher will bring a bucket of water and a scuttle of coal for the day's session.
3) Make your pens carefully. You may whittle nibs to the individual taste of the pupils.
4) Men teachers may take 1 evening each week for courting purposes, or 2 evenings a week if they go to church regularly.
5) After 10 hours in school, the teachers may spend the remaining time reading the Bible or other good books.
6) Women teachers who marry or engage in unseemly conduct will be dismissed.
7) Every teacher should lay aside from each pay a goodly sum of his earnings for his benefit during his declining years so that he will not become a burden on society.
8) Any teacher who smokes, uses liquor in any form, frequents pool or public halls, or gets shaved in a barber shop will give good reason to suspect his worth, intention, integrity, and honesty.
9) The teacher who performs his labor faithfully and without fault for 5 years will be given an increase of 25¢ per week in his pay, providing the Board of Education approves.

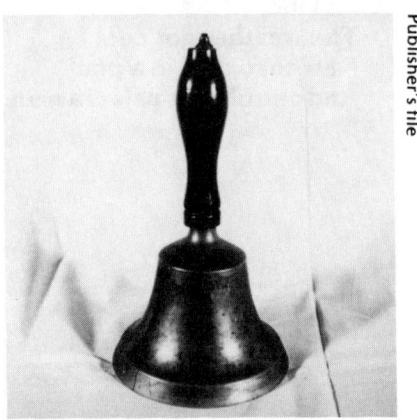

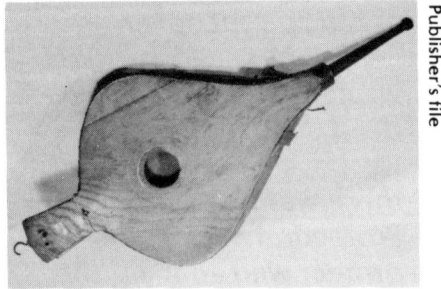

A LESSON IN LOYALTY

The story of Damon and Pythias is a classical folktale about two friends who lived in Syracuse during the reign of the military tyrant and ruler, Dionysius the Elder. Between the years 405-375 B.C. Dionysius waged three wars against Carthage and he was known as one of the most brutal military leaders of the times.

But even the most brutal can be touched by a very special kind of friendship.

Dionysius had condemned Pythias to death. Damon, Pythias' best friend, offered himself to Dionysius as a hostage while Pythias went home to settle his affairs before his execution.

Just as the hour of execution came, Pythias returned to release his friend from hostage and face his own death.

Centuries later, the spirit of that special friendship became the symbol of an organization in Canada called "The Knights of Pythias." It was a charitable organization offering a helping hand to others. Today, it concentrates its help on the needs of cerebral palsy sufferers.

Dionysius had never seen such loyalty between friends. He was SO impressed that he pardoned Pythias and asked for the honor of being a friend of theirs.

Daddy for 25¢ for a box of Reeves paints but Mama was horrified that I would want to waste money on such nonsense.

The teachers were strict then, especially if you were cheeky in class or caught sliding down the railings by the school steps. You would get the strap. The School Board finally had bolts put in the railings to stop us sliding down them.

It didn't really matter when you went to school in Vancouver, there were always some children who would cause trouble. Like Joe, who broke the top off the hydrant. Somebody said he should be locked in a dungeon. Somebody else said that he should be locked up and put on bread and water. Putting him in a dungeon would have terrified him but the bread and water would have been OK. It would have helped him lose some weight.

Some children, especially in the primaries, would be bad and not really know it. Like the grade 2 student caught stealing. The school had been losing pencils and paper and rulers and things. This little grade 2 student was caught. He had some pencils on him. Well, the teacher called the principal and he asked him, "What else did you take?"

Of course, we all expected him to say, "Nothing!" But do you know what he said?

"Everything else that's missing."

He was so innocent about it. His parents were having a hard time so he didn't get the strap. But he had to bring everything back.

Most of the children, though, were good. We liked the teachers. My favourite was Miss Stacey. She was so pretty in her crisp white frilly blouse and long black sweeping skirt. She always wore her hair up. That was how I wanted to wear my hair but Mama always put it in braids and ribbons.

It was Miss Stacey who formed our choir and entered us in the music festival run by the Knights of Pythias. That was a charitable organization started in the 1800s to help others. Its name comes from the legend of Damon and Pythias.

There was one group from the east end. They were nearly all Oriental children and they sang and acted out "Bobby Shafto's Gone to Sea." One of the adjudicators

When is an island not really an island?

Granville Island isn't really an island. It is a man-made peninsula. In 1888, the first Granville Street bridge—a wooden trestle—spanned False Creek. In that year, work began reclaiming land along the eastern end of False Creek where industries could be set up.

In September, 1909, the second Granville Street bridge opened. By 1917, the area that would be Granville Island had been dyked and filled.

By 1920, it had become the centre of industry in that city. There were sawmills, processing plants, warehouses, gravel dumps, foundries, and hog-fuel burners all cluttered into the reclaimed area.

For the next 3 decades, the area clattered and sparked with industrial work. But, as the city expanded and industries moved, the area became abandoned.

It would have stayed that way if it hadn't been for 2 men by the name of Bill Harvey and Mitch Taylor who converted the old Monsanto Chemical factory to the now famous Mulvaney's Restaurant.

Another man, Ron Basford, began a move to transfer the control of Granville Island from the National Harbours Board to the Canada Mortgage and Housing Corporation and form the Granville Island Trust. As a result, Granville Island was transformed from an abandoned industrial site to one of Vancouver's best loved and internationally known shopping, eating, and entertaining centres.

In December, 1887, the city's first library, the Vancouver Reading Room, opened above Thomas Dunn's hardware store on Cordova Street. A year later, the bylaws of the room were changed so that women could use it.

On December 5, 1889, the Imperial Opera House staged the city's first Shakesperean production: Richard III.

The Vancouver Stock Exchange opened in 1907.

The CBC began broadcasting in Vancouver in 1953.

The Empire Stadium opened in 1954.

The Maritime Museum and the Queen Elizabeth Theatre opened in 1959.

The H. R. MacMillan Planetarium and the Centennial Museum opened in 1968.

was Scottish and I can still hear his broad Scottish accent when he said, "That's the first time I've seen a Japanese Navy!" Every child was dressed like a sailor!

We took our lunches to school, just like you do. I took bread and jam or a peanut butter sandwich. Our neighbours made their own peanut butter. I took gingerbread, too. We drank water from the school fountain. We didn't have wax paper or saran wrap in those days so we wrapped our lunches in napkins. The trouble was, all the flavours ran! Have you ever had cake tasting of fish sandwich? Or spice-flavoured bread and jam? YUCK! Some children took their lunches in tin cans and the country kids used lard pails.

We didn't have Physical Education then. Our teachers thought we'd get all the running around we needed during recess and lunch. But we did do some exercises standing in the aisles between our desks.

The idea of a university began in 1899. That was when the Vancouver High School also became a college linked with McGill University in Montreal. The very first college class had only 6 students! In 1906, the college was renamed McGill University College of B.C. In 1912, it moved to some buildings on the grounds of the Vancouver General Hospital. In 1915, the college closed and the University of B.C. opened using the same buildings. But it was not until 1925 when the University moved to Point Grey.

The 1930s were difficult years. Because of the Depression, high school students stayed in school longer. There were no jobs for them. But, in 1939, when war in Europe broke out, there were more jobs because

U.B.C. Campus 1925.

3) I spy with my little eye
A track weaving round
through the trees
full of wolves, deer, and sheep
and beaver who'll peep
at you going for a ride
in the breeze.

During World War II, the Japanese and their families were sent to the Okanagan to work in camps. These children were known as "evacuees" because they were evacuated (sent away) from Vancouver.

of the "war industries" and students left to get work.

In 1940, the School Board brought in military cadet training for teenagers between 14 and 18 years of age. They had to participate in military drill and target practice. Some of the students thought it was a great change from math but some didn't like it at all. Secretly, it scared me. I wondered if the war was coming to Canada. But it never did, even though I knew of lots of men who left Vancouver to fight in Europe.

The Vancouver School Board tried hard to protect the really good students from going to war. In 1942, the board and the University of B.C. suggested that good students might be allowed to withhold from enlisting in the Armed Forces.

Actually, 1942 was a terrible year. On December 7, 1941, the Japanese had dropped bombs on the military

The first European to come to the British Columbia coast was the Spanish explorer, Juan Perez, Captain of the **Santiago.** *Perez discovered the Queen Charlotte Islands and anchored at the entrance of Nootka Sound on the west coast of Vancouver Island in 1774.*

The Americas as they were known in 1741.

Provincial Archives, Victoria

The Hon. John Robson's home.

Robson Street is named after the Hon. John Robson who succeeded Alexander Davie as premier. In the months before British Columbia became a province in 1871, Robson fought for what he called "responsible government"—provincial governments that were allowed to manage their own affairs.

Powell Street is named after Dr. Israel Wood Powell. His name is also given to a street in Victoria and Powell River on the mainland. Dr. Powell helped to set up the public school system and was the second superintendent of schools.

station in Pearl Harbor in Hawaii. This is what brought the war in Europe to the North Pacific. All of us in Vancouver were terrified of what would happen. There were blackouts and military alerts and all the Japanese in the city were rounded up as dangerous enemy aliens and sent to work in camps in the Okanagan Valley in the B.C. interior.

All the Japanese children went, too. The number of students in school dropped until other families moved into the areas of the city where the Japanese used to live. Their children replaced the missing Japanese children and the number of children in school went up again.

A lot of students from grades 9 to 12 took a 5-month summer leave from school during 1942. They were allowed to do that if they could prove they had work in the valley working for the farmers. But they had to put in extra hours of study in school before leaving and they had to take a special course when they returned in November to catch up.

Every school played some kind of sport. There was soccer, rugby, and basketball. Some schools had only 1 or 2 soccer balls to be shared among all 8 grades in the school. Nobody had all the protective clothing children wear today. You just played in what you were wearing.

Some schools had vocational time. One afternoon or morning a week, the girls studied domestic science where they learned to cook. The boys had manual training where they learned to use tools in the workshop.

Most of us wore the same kind of clothes to school. The girls wore skirts and blouses. Sometimes I wore my favourite blue serge uniform which was like a dress with a blouse underneath. The boys wore jackets, shirts, and trousers and we all had strong walking shoes.

In the 1960s, though, what teenagers wore to school became quite an argument. You see, a girl had gone to school in North Vancouver wearing the latest miniskirt, a tight-fitting top, and her hair back-combed so much it looked like a bird's nest. The principal sent her home and her parents were really angry with him. She ended up going to another school. The School Board set up a code of dress for all students.

Actually, you didn't HAVE to wear clothes according to the code. It was voluntary but most of the students obeyed it.

THE CASE OF BILLY BUTT-INSKY

Score: Billy Goat 1
Police Officer 0

Even though the 1930s were difficult years, there was always something happening to make you laugh. Like the day of the butting billy goat encounter.

It was just before 9:00 a.m. on a chilly morning in early February, 1936. Children were rushing to school. Grownups were going to work. On the corner of Cassiar and Hastings Streets, a bossy billy goat was having fun playing a game of bullfight with the children.

No matter what they did, he kept charging them. The children dodged and tried to run around him but all they got were butts in the behinds.

The police were called and Officer Washbrook arrived on his motorcycle. Well, the goat took one look at THAT mechanical animal and geared up for a REAL challenge!

With the threat shifted from the children to the bike, the children relaxed and began to enjoy a real show as goat and bike charged in open offence.

Just as the officer swerved at the last minute, the goat ploughed into the sidecar with a crack that could be heard blocks away.

By now, everyone was cheering. Not for the officer. For the goat!

Just as the goat slowed to catch its breath, Officer Washbrook got ready to leap the animal in true police-style grand finale.

But it didn't happen quite that way. The officer leaped forward. The goat leaped sideways. The 2 collided in midair, rolled on the ground and scrambled for footing. Of course, the goat was faster and in no time, to the cheers of the growing crowd, he was standing over the officer, glowering with triumph!

By now the event was becoming the spectacle of the town. A garageman ran to help the officer and a police car swooped onto the scene.

In a three-on-one tussle, the cheers were for the goat, though the game was over from the start.

But that wasn't the end of the fun.

With the goat under control, the 2 officers couldn't decide what to do with it. No way was the patrolman going to have the thing on the back seat of his car. And no way could the goat go tandem on the motorcycle.

Finally, Officer Washbrook, exhausted and disgruntled, loaded the indignant goat into his sidecar, ordered the garageman to sit on top of it, and roared off to the local police station. He likely spent the rest of the day doing pooper-scooper duty in the goat's jail cell...

DRESS CODE FOR STUDENTS, 1962

Do's for Girls:
   Below-the-knee skirts
   Jumper or tailored dresses
   Cotton blouses
   Cardigans and pullover sweaters
   Ankle or knee-length socks
   Oxford loafers or saddle shoes.

Do's for Boys:
   Shirt and tie or open neck sports shirt
   Cardigan or pullover
   Blazer or sports jacket
   Flannel, corduroy, drill or cotton pants
   Oxford loafers
   Boots are all right if prescribed by a doctor.

Don'ts for Girls:
   Extreme hair-do's
   Any make-up other than neutral shade lipstick
   Sheer blouses and dresses
   Short, ugly skirts or slacks of any kind
   Figure-emphasizing sweaters
   High-heeled, open-toed or sandal shoes
   Nylons will be frowned upon before Grade 10.

Don'ts for Boys:
   T-shirts
   Sweat shirts
   Wind jackets
   Blue jeans
   Overalls.

Sunday afternoon on the bikes!

3. Having Fun!

What better place is there ANYWHERE than Vancouver for having fun! If Daddy wasn't taking us for walks along the river or up the mountains, Mama was taking us to the beach to make sandcastles or to Stanley Park for picnics.

When Billy, my younger brother, was still a baby, he was fussy and used to cry a lot. So, to help him settle down, Mama used to take us to Sunset Beach where John and I would go swimming and draw in the sand and Billy would sleep in his buggy. Well, that was what he was SUPPOSED to do.

I can remember one day when all he did was howl all the way. A friend of Mama's lived not too far from the beach so, while John and I went exploring and crab collecting, Mama took Billy to Mrs. James' house to have a cup of tea and change Billy's clothes.

We had a great time. There were all kinds of crabs to collect as well as pretty shells the seagulls had picked clean when the tide had gone out.

John chased me across the beach with a slithery piece of seaweed but I got even with him by stuffing it down his back when he wasn't looking.

After going for a swim, we decided to join Mama at Mrs. James' house. I still swear, to this day, if John had carried the bucket of crabs like I asked him to instead of me, nothing would have happened.

You see, I was so excited about all the crabs we had collected that, when we got to Mrs. James' house, I didn't stop running even when we went inside. There was carpet everywhere! I'd never seen so many carpets and every one of them had tassels on the ends.

But, at first, because I was running so hard, I didn't see the tassels. I didn't mean to catch my toe in the tassels but, when I did, I did the neatest belly-flop on the carpet I've ever done in my life. Me, the carpet, and the bucket of crabs took off in the fastest, nose-flattening skid I've ever done and 10 zillion crabs took off in 10 zillion directions all over the room.

Mama told me later that I let out such a howl that it stopped Billy's howl right in mid-screech. It was the first time he'd stopped crying all day. But, she said, with my noise the house wasn't any quieter.

Have you ever seen a room ALIVE with crabs? I mean, everywhere you looked there was a crab having a spazz-attack trying to find the beach. I didn't dare look at Mrs. James' face. But I knew what she was doing because I could hear the sobs. I didn't even glance at Mama's face.

It took the rest of the day to pick up the crabs and clean up. By then, Billy was howling again and we STILL had to walk all the way home.

It was ages before we went back to Mrs. James' house. It wasn't until I was grown up when I figured out why Mama changed her routine and only visited her friends' houses when we were in school.

Sunday was the day most families did things together. That was because all the fathers worked the rest of the week and were too tired to do anything but sit at home on the weekday evenings. On Sundays, families would go to the beach or to Stanley Park for a picnic and visit the zoo or go to friends' houses to visit.

The first bicycle in Vancouver was a "boneshaker" imported in 1888 by Bob Matheson, who ran a print shop on Hastings Street.

The "safety bicycle" was introduced in the 1890s. The first one imported from England appeared in Vancouver in 1891.

The first cycle club organized in Vancouver was the Vancouver Bicycle Club established in 1891. In March, 1892, it had 209 members.

4) I spy with my little eye
a place where one world
meets another,
which we see now and then
if we're willing to spend
an hour or two locked under
cover.

Crazy George made music

As much as children loved to play, they loved getting to know some of the more unusual characters in town.

Like Crazy George.

His real name was George Dyer and he had been raised as a polite English gentleman. He lived by himself in a one-room shack at the edge of town in what would be Mount Pleasant.

But he wasn't harmful at all. He was shabby but clean and his hair was long, white, and silky. Because he was so friendly when he DID come out of his shack—which wasn't often—children would run and meet him and ask to help him with something.

It was his habit of talking to "voices" that gave him the name "Crazy George." He didn't say just a few words either. He'd have whole arguments that went on for hours with these imaginary demons! People would hear him shouting when he was inside his shack and the door closed.

continued on page 33

The rest of the week, children were left to make their own fun. And did we ever!

Most of the boys went fishing or swimming or played ball. The girls spent a lot of time playing with their dolls. I loved my dolls. They weren't the plastic, real-life kind you play with today. They were made of china with baby-like faces and chubby legs and arms.

Suzie, my best friend, had a brown-haired doll. Mine had fair hair and we both had doll buggies. One summer, we tried to make cupola shades for our buggies like the real baby buggies but they were too difficult so we made shades with wooden boards and supporting sticks. They were sort of like the surrey with the fringe on top in the movie "Oklahoma."

Of course, we made other things too. We made dolls' beds and boxes for their clothes and covers and we even tried to make a doll house but that was too adventurous for us.

Daddy helped us with that project and Mama made tiny lace curtains for the cut-out windows. We made wood and paper furniture and spent days figuring out how to fold the stiff paper and cut everything just right to make chairs, tables, bed, and bureaux.

I must have had an obsession with candy when I was a little girl. I can remember, one day, Mama was really cross. I can't remember what it was about but she told me, "There's a lickin' in store for you, Mary-Margaret."

Well, the next time we went to the store, I looked EVERYWHERE for this "licking," thinking it was candy. Stores, like schools, were painted in a gloomy brown and this store always seemed so dark and forbidding. But I was determined to find the "licking."

I could see a barrel down a dark aisle and it took all my courage to creep down it while Mama was shopping and peak inside the barrel. It was full of ginger snaps! How I loved ginger snaps and I couldn't wait to tell Mama I'd found the "licking" and would she buy some. That was when I found out that the "licking" Mama was talking about wasn't the one I was hoping for. . . .

Shopping was always fun, especially at Christmas time. Mama let me help a lot with Christmas shopping. She would give me a whole dollar bill, and for one dollar, I could buy 6 really lovely gifts. Of course, this was back in

Spencer's—Then and now!

the early 1900s when things didn't cost as much as they do today. I mean, 5¢ would buy you toy trumpets, drums or toy carpet sweepers and things like that.

I can remember some more excitement going shopping. Daddy started it all. No, actually, it was the store called Spencer's on Hastings Street that started it. They put in a moving stair. You call them an escalator now. Back then, nobody in the whole WORLD had heard of a moving stair! Daddy took us all to Spencer's that evening to see this marvel. All the other dads in the city must have had the same idea because Spencer's was

Crazy George made music

continued from page 32

He never did let anyone help him, though. Not even when he went to draw water from a nearby tap and carry it back to his shack in two large, trimmed-off coal-oil tins. He would suspend them from an old broom handle laid across his shoulders just like the way a Chinese peddler carries his vegetables.

No one knew if he ever had a job. But one thing he could do was play a flute. Children used to listen to him for hours. His fingers were so nimble and light on the instrument that the notes sounded like birdsong. Listening to his musical talent, no one would have thought there was anything wrong with the world.

But there was something wrong with his world. Some great sadness. Some people said that he had been jilted by an English girl when he was younger. No one knew for sure. No one knew ANYTHING about him for sure except that he lived by himself, played his flute and argued with the voices only he could hear...

The thrill of the circus!

Vancouver City Archives

The creek, the fire, the fun!

A place where children always used to play in Vancouver was on the banks of a creek called Brewery Creek. This creek drained into False Creek near East First Avenue and Scotia Street.

Called "the Ravine" by most children in the area, the creek flowed through forest stands of cedar and fir at the turn of the century. Berry bushes and grasses sheltered its banks and the waters were as much fun for families of ducks as they were for the children who fished, swam, and waded in the shallows.

For children like Mary-Margaret, Suzie, John and Billy, the creek was a playground, a forest retreat, a fairyland, and a fort. It was a place to gather violets, mayflowers, ferns, and mosses. It was a place to snack on "sasky" and "much-a-muck," (the new shoots of the salmon berry and thimble berry bushes) salal berries, licorice root, raspberries, blueberries, huckleberries, and blackberries.

It was a place to watch out for devils club and skunk cabbage, stinging nettles, and bees' nests.

It was a place to dream, play make-believe, and share secrets high up in the trees where the crows cawed and the robins laid their tiny blue eggs.

continued on page 35

just crammed with people! Actually, that made it more exciting.

We had to wait in turn to try the stairs, and by the time we could go on it, Billy was almost beside himself with excitement. There was a man standing guard at the bottom of the moving stairs and another man at the top. Mama thought the cleets were made of maple wood but I didn't care what they were made of. I just wanted to ride on it. And ride it we children did! Lining up time and time again to go on the moving stairs.

I suppose that seems pretty silly now, with almost every department store having escalators and elevators and almost every gadget electronically operated. But, in the early 1900s, the real wonder of the modern age was just dawning and the simplest things were marvels to

"Black Joe"

The creek, the fire, the fun!

continued from page 34

And it was a place to watch a little bit of history pass by. For, near where the creek drained into False Creek, two slaughterhouses stood. About 1904, the two slaughterhouse firms moved from their locations by the creek to new industrial sites.

Under the supervision of the Vancouver Fire Brigade, the slaughterhouse buildings were ordered burned.

All the children of the area watched, fascinated, as the buildings were torched. Within moments, something else happened they hadn't anticipated.

All the rats—big ones, little ones, and the hundred or so in-between ones—scuttled from the buildings and took to the waters of the creek to swim to the safety of the cowfields beyond.

While the grownups were alarmed and disgusted, the children were fascinated! It was a real Pied Piper story and who better to be Vancouver's Pied Piper than Vancouver's fire chief!

With the slaughterhouses gone, life along the banks of Brewery Creek settled back into tranquility again, until the march of progress saw the forest, the berry bushes, and the banks of the stream disappear as Vancouver grew and spread.

children—and grownups—living in cities like Vancouver.

As children we were easily excited. Like when the circus came to town. Now THAT was real excitement with all those trained wild animals and big top tents and clowns and high wire acts and the beautiful ladies riding bareback on prancing horses.

The circus was Barnham and Bailey. Buffalo Bill and Annie Oakley were a part of it. Annie Oakley was doing a fabulous western act, standing on a circling horse, shooting at balls.

The circus back then had 3 rings, not just one, and it was a major summer event. Before opening night, all the performers and animals would parade through the streets of Vancouver. It sure looked funny to see elephants and bareback riders and clowns on stilts go down Hastings Street behind cages of lions and tigers! Then there were bands and more clowns and the ring master himself.

Every child in town lined up to watch the circus parade. Then they pestered their parents to take them to the show. How John, Billy, and I loved it and I vowed, secretly, after seeing Annie Oakley, that, when I grew up, I would be a bareback rider!

While the circus was the highlight of summer, swimming was what we did nearly every day. We would

The Vancouver Symphony Orchestra. — Vancouver Symphony Society

Bringing music to the city...

The idea of Vancouver having its own Symphony Orchestra began in 1897 when 23 musicians began rehearsing together above a hardware store. Led by Music Director Adolf Gregory, the young VSO held its first concert in Dunn Hall on November 11, 1897.

But, after only 3 concerts, the orchestra died because of lack of money. For the next 30 years, people tried to start another symphony orchestra but the only one that did get formed was a 40-member orchestra led by Oscar Ziegler in 1915. It disbanded after he died in 1917.

It wasn't until 1930 when the next Vancouver Symphony Orchestra was started. A lady called Mrs. B. T. Rogers provided the money to get it going and the musicians were drawn from Vancouver's theatres, nightclubs, and radio studios.

The new VSO had 70 musicians and its first concert was held on October 5, 1930, in the Orpheum Theatre. They played Beethoven's Fifth Symphony.

Its second concert was held on December 7, 1930. It featured Russian-born pianist Jan Cherniavsky. From then on, the orchestra became more and more popular.

The years during the Second World War were difficult. From 1940 to 1946 the orchestra was without a conductor. But it enjoyed some internationally famous visiting conductors who led the orchestra through some memorable, musical times. They included Sir John Barbirolli, Sir Ernest MacMillan, Leonard Bernstein, Sir Thomas Beecham, and Otto Klemperer.

In 1952, Irwin Hoffman became the orchestra's conductor and he stayed with the VSO until 1964. It was under his leadership that the orchestra began touring the province of British Columbia. It was he who conducted the orchestra's first concert in the Queen Elizabeth Theatre in 1959.

In 1972, Kazuyoshi Akiyama became music director and principal conductor. Under his leadership, the orchestra became famous around the world. In 1974, the orchestra made its first tour abroad when it visited 6 centres in Japan. In 1976, it was the first major symphony orchestra to tour Canada.

take the tram car to Jericho Beach and spend nearly all day in the water.

Jericho Beach is part of English Bay, and in the early 1900s a very special man took it upon himself to watch out for the children who swam there. He was a black man and his name was Joe Fortes but everybody called him "Black Joe."

He taught all kinds of children to swim and there was always a lineup of children shouting "Me next! Me next!" He was THAT popular.

Back in the early 1900s when Black Joe was teaching children to swim, the beach was divided by a huge boulder at the foot of Denman Street. The rule was: All women bathed in the water to the west of it and all men swam to the east of it. Women didn't have bikinis and swim suits like they do today. Their bathing suits looked like dresses and they even wore tights and sandals to swim in. Well, one day, a young lady decided to go swimming without her tights on. We all saw her. She was bare naked right up to her knees! What a flap everyone got into. Mama tried to hide Billy's eyes but he just howled with laughter. Mama thought it was disgraceful and the Women's Christian Temperance Union wrote to the paper about her. Well, the lady must have had spunk because she sued the union for libel. The case went to court and she was awarded damages.

The beach was always a place of activity. In the summer, there's the annual bathtub race from Nanaimo

Mamas and daddies on a Sunday picnic, on the SS Princess May.

Provincial Archives, Victoria

Anyone for a hair-do? Grooming time at the P.N.E.

Vancouver on display: The PNE

When the first Exhibition was held at Hastings Park in August, 1910, there weren't any streetcars that went that far east. A special train was made available by the C.P.R. and visitors from Vancouver could go by boat to Exhibition Wharf.

The first exhibition featured horse, dog, and poultry shows as well as industrial and agricultural exhibits. There was a free Vaudeville show in front of the grandstand and there were wrestling competitions, snake charmers, Dutch comedians, Salome dancers, African dodgers, sandwich and lemonade stands, and a tobacconist's stand selling cigars.

The exhibition promoted arts and crafts as well as industries. There were displays of tapestries, embroideries, oil paintings, pen drawings, and mounted birds by local taxidermists. There were children's works, too—displays of furniture pieces made by pupils at the manual training school.

The first exhibition was opened by Prime Minister Sir Wilfrid Laurier. Sixty-eight thousand people attended it. Since then, an exhibition has been held every year with the exception of the war years (1942-1946).

In 1843, the Hudson's Bay Company set up Fort Victoria on Vancouver Island which later became its headquarters.

In 1866, Vancouver Island united with the mainland colony of British Columbia. In 1868, the capital was moved from New Westminster to Victoria.

In 1886, Canada's population was 4.6 million.

In 1886, Vancouver's population rose from around 600 to 1,000 people.

The Hudson's Bay Company opened its first Vancouver store in January, 1887.

In 1891, the first Woodward's store opened its doors on Georgia Street and Westminster Avenue, later called Main Street.

In 1894, a cannon was set up at Brockton Point. It was fired every evening at 6:00 p.m. to mark the time that fishing had to stop. Later it was changed to 9:00 p.m. and it was known as the nine o'clock gun.

In 1909, the city's first skyscraper was finished. It was the Dominion Trust Building on the corner of Hastings and Cambie Streets. It was 13 storeys high.

In 1910, an electric railway line was built on the south bank of the Fraser River from Chilliwack to New Westminster. It connected with a tramline to Vancouver. Farmers shipped their dairy products, fruits, vegetables, and meats from the Fraser Valley to New Westminster via this new railway. The daily run became known as the "milk special."

to Vancouver, and in the winter, there's the crazy Polar Bear swim. This started on January 1, 1921, and Daddy and all of us children would take part in it just for fun. The year the water was the coldest was in 1925 when it was only 3°C and the air temperature at 0°C. That WAS frosty!

Winter time was fun though, especially when we went to the toboggan hills. Despite what people think, Vancouver does get snow, and in the early days, we had LOTS of it. Every neighbourhood had a toboggan hill and they could stretch for the length of 7 to 10 city blocks. No wonder the toboggan rides were such fun!

Making a toboggan was a family event and they would be big enough to hold the whole family. There would be a small sleigh at the front and back of the toboggan, a long plank to sit on and a foot rail and it was nothing to see a family of 10 come whizzing down the hill at a crazy speed with the dad steering in front and Mama hanging on for dear life at the back with all the children squealing in the middle!

There were all kinds of group outings year-round, organized by either a Sunday School or the company where the fathers worked. There would be trips to parks in the city or special places in the Fraser Valley such as Fort Langley, Harrison Hot Springs or a farm. There

May Day, 1906.

The thrill of a night time: The Orpheum

People dressed so elegantly when they went to the Opera at The Orpheum.

When the Orpheum Theatre was built in 1927, its architect, B. Marcus Priteca, described it as "conservative Spanish Renaissance." It glittered with colour schemes of gold and ivory. There was gold leaf on the pilasters and colonnades, silk wallpaper on the walls, and maroon velvet curtains draped across windows. The hall was lit by 100 glittering chandeliers and the main ones were made of hand-crafted Czechoslovakian crystal.

Opening night of The Orpheum was THE social event of the year. The opening film was a silent one called "THE WISE WIFE" and it starred Phyllis Haver. There was a stage show, too, featuring Marie White and the Blue Slickers, Chaney and Fox "Delight Dance Delineators," Ethel Davis in "refreshing song chatter," and Toto the Clown.

The new theatre had 3,000 seats and was the largest on the Pacific coast. World famous entertainers performed there including Charlie Chaplin, Bob Hope, and ballerina Margot Fonteyn.

In 1939, The Orpheum was taken over by Famous Players Theatres. In 1970, Famous Players wanted to completely remodel The Orpheum and convert it into several mini-theatres.

But, because The Orpheum was so much a part of Vancouver's history, a lot of people felt it would be a great loss to see it turned into mini-theatres. They persuaded the City of Vancouver to approach Famous Players and try to buy it from them. As a result, the city bought The Orpheum for $3.9 million. They then raised enough money to renovate it as an historic building.

The same man who had originally worked on The Orpheum in 1927 came back to work on its renovation. He was Tony Heinsbergen. He supervised the interior decoration.

In his studio, he painted the canvasses for the mural. The mural was applied to the dome, which was about 18 metres high. He finished the mural by hand. He had to stand on scaffolding and he was helped by assistants.

The architects also contracted Italian-born Joseph Tinucci who had studied at the Florentine Art School in Italy. He renovated the decorative plasterwork.

Today, The Orpheum is a monument to the history of Vancouver.

Dunsmuir Street is named after the 2 Dunsmuirs of the famous Dunsmuir family of Vancouver Island. When Lauchlan Hamilton began the task of naming Vancouver's streets, he named the street after Robert Dunsmuir, the mining baron. But many people associate the street with Robert's son, James, who was appointed lieutenant governor in 1906. James Dunsmuir died in 1920. He was believed to be the richest man in B.C. with a wealth of $3 million.

would be berry picking trips and Mama would bottle the berries or make jam with them later. We would go on outings to have races and games, or boat trips to places like the Sunshine Coast.

Some families went camping for a few days and others visited relatives or friends.

Just like children everywhere, we played all the usual games such as hopscotch, hide-and-go-seek, tag (which some children called run-sheep-run), cowboys and Indians, Robinson Crusoe, jacks, skipping, and hoops. Everybody roller-skated. Vancouver had its first roller-skating rink by the end of 1886 but, later, when people had radios, teenagers used to put the radios against the windows of their houses, turn the music up loud and roller skate in the street.

On the May 24 weekend, we would go to New Westminster to see the crowning of the May Queen. Suzie wanted to be a May Queen one day and, secretly, so did I. But I didn't think I would ever be as pretty as the "Queens" we saw being crowned. But we used to pretend anyway! When we got home, Suzie and I used to gather long thin blades of grass and weave them into our own crowns, filling them up with dandelions.

Sometimes, having fun wasn't so much DOING something as it was having a laugh. Like the time when

Homer Street was named after J. A. R. Homer who owned the first sawmill on the Lower Fraser and was one of the province's first exporters of lumber.

The Vancouver Symphony Orchestra in the Orpheum Theatre in 1918.

Mama had this brilliant idea of making a rockery in front of our house. I don't think Daddy thought it was such a good idea but we all helped him do it under Mama's instructions anyway. We spent a WHOLE weekend digging out a hole where the rockery was going to be. Before filling it with rocks and soil, Daddy layered the bottom with some dead salmon for fertilizer.

"They'll make the soil good an' rich so Mama's plants'll grow," he told us.

But something happened before Mama's plants even got planted. During the night, the smell of the salmon wafted into the forest. A couple of bears smelled it, and of course, you can guess what they did. By morning the bears had not only dug up the rockery but the entire garden! They'd been no more than 4 feet from our front door and not one of us had heard a thing!

In the early days, when Vancouver was still surrounded by forest, bears were always visiting the city, looking for goodies—like Mr. Hatch's laying chickens or Mrs. Jackson's clothes line or the rows of garbage at the local dump.

Cows could be a problem too. There was a large field of cabbages at the end of our street and a cow got in and ate them all. Mr. Smith, the cabbage grower, wasn't very happy about that.

Lots of people had their own cow back then. Even our neighbour. Once Mama caught Billy riding the thing down the middle of the street! He was just as proud as could be sitting up there in his blue denim overalls and old blue shirt. The cow was as white as Mama's apron with the biggest, fullest udder I'd ever seen in my life. It didn't walk. It waddled.

Mama made Billy take the cow right back to our neighbour's house and it was just as well because I don't think the cow could have waddled any further. It was mooing so sadly Billy had to milk it straight away. He didn't mind though. He milked the cow for the neighbour every day and got paid a nickel for the chore. Mama sometimes bought milk from the neighbour when she didn't buy it from the delivery man.

There were always things to do, things to see, and things to laugh at when we wanted to have fun but sometimes it was fun just to be alone.

Sir James Douglas

James Douglas was the first governor of British Columbia. He was sworn in at Fort Langley in 1858. He moved to New Westminster when that settlement was made the colony's capital in 1859.

The "Lions"—Peaks of a Legend.

My favourite "alone" place was my little attic bedroom. I liked to sit by the window with my favourite doll and look out over the city at the towering mountains on the North Shore.

The most famous peaks are the "Lions." They are what Lions Gate Bridge is named after. When I was very young I used to think that they were the Lions because lions lived up there! That used to scare me and I used to wonder how long it would take for them to come down the mountain, swim across Burrard Inlet, cross the city and Granville Street Bridge then walk down Seventh Avenue to my house. I would figure it would take them all night by which time Mama and Daddy would be up and they would take care of the lions and all of us children would be safe.

Of course, there weren't any lions living up there! The peaks were called that because somebody thought they looked like the stone lions that guard Nelson's column in Trafalgar Square in London, England.

The Indians, though, knew the peaks as "Checheyohee" (The Twins). Their legend says that 2 sisters wanted to invite their people's enemy to their coming-of-age celebration which their father, a great chief, was putting on for them.

When the war canoes arrived, they weren't filled with weapons but gifts. The celebration was the most successful one they had ever had. At the end of it the

The earliest Indians to inhabit southwest British Columbia were the Pebble Indians. They hunted and trapped small and big game animals as well as whales, seals, and otters.
Their culture and society developed quickly. By the time the first Europeans arrived, the Indian nations had become complex and sophisticated. In the area that is now greater Vancouver, there were about 5,000 Indians living in villages near the water. They were the Musqueam and the Squamish.

chief's daughters were lifted up and set in a high place so that everybody would remember that they had helped them all honour the 2 most precious feelings: peace and brotherhood. The Lions peaks today are still thought of as the twin peaks of peace and brotherly love.

That's the sort of thing that makes Vancouver so special.

The Indians fascinated me. Alone in my attic, I'd wonder what it would be like to be an Indian girl and live in cedar huts like they did. Some of their homes, though, were the longhouses and families lived together inside them. I used to wonder if all the children played together all the time or if they had special places where they could be alone like me.

The Indians were great hunters and fishermen and there were always clamshells around Indian villages. In fact, the first roads in Stanley Park were paved with scrunched clamshells. They looked so pretty. They were always white because of the colour of the shell, and after it had rained, the road around Stanley Park was the cleanest, shiniest and whitest in the whole city.

Daddy once said the road to Heaven was paved with gold. That's silly, I thought. The road to Heaven should be paved with clamshells, and there should be maple trees arching across it. You should be able to hear the waves from Burrard Inlet and see the eagles and the seagulls circling above. And, when you got to Heaven, you should be able to see the Lions peaks of peace and brotherhood.

Because, as I grew up and had fun in the young city, Vancouver, to me, was like Heaven on Earth.

THIS CITY HAS FIVE SISTERS

What is a Sister City?

For Vancouver, a sister city is another city in the world with which it has a cultural, festive, economic, or geographic tie.

Vancouver has five sister cities. They are: Odessa in the U.S.S.R.; Edinburgh in Scotland; Yokohama in Japan; Guangzhou in China; and Los Angeles in California, U.S.A.

Vancouver twinned (became a sister city) with Odessa for sentimental reasons. During the Second World War, Canadian merchant ships used to go into the port of Odessa to shelter from enemy attack.

Vancouver twinned with Edinburgh because, like herself, the Scottish capital is a festive city.

Vancouver twinned with Yokohama because both cities are Pacific Rim cities that have traded with each other for many years.

Vancouver twinned with Guangzhou for historical reasons. Guangzhou used to be called Canton and many Chinese immigrants came to Vancouver from Canton in the early days.

Vancouver twinned with Los Angeles because both these west coast North American cities share many cultural, economic, and historical ties.

Indian homes on Burrard Inlet. Provincial Archives, Victoria

4. Growing Up is Hard to Do

Of course, life wasn't ALL fun and games. There were difficult times too. Sometimes, there were very hard times.

Even before Vancouver was born, there were epidemics that killed lots of people, especially Indians. For instance, the smallpox epidemic of 1862. Back then, explorers and traders regularly came from San Francisco to Victoria. Many Indians camped near Victoria because of all the trading of furs, liquor, guns, and goods. In 1862, there were Tlingit, Haida, Tsimshian, Nootka, and Salish Indians all keeping the peace and trading with the white people.

The smallpox virus was brought from San Francisco by a visitor who had become ill on board ship. The virus spread like mad through Victoria, especially among the Indians. Within 2 years, thousands of natives had died from it.

It was cruel, how they died. Because people were so

Nelson Street is named after Hugh Nelson who became lieutenant governor on February 8, 1887. During his office, he had the distinction of swearing in 3 British Columbia premiers: Alexander Davie, John Robson, and Theodore Davie (the younger brother of Alexander).

Granville Street is named after the town's original name, Granville, which had been named after Lord Granville, the distinguished English statesman of Queen Victoria's time.

Comox Street takes its name from the city of Comox on Vancouver Island. The word "comox" comes from an Indian word, "komuckway" meaning "land of plenty."

Burrard Street is named after Captain Vancouver's naval friend, Sir Harry Burrard.

afraid of the disease, those who were sick were left alone in the woods to die. Some were tied to trees or abandoned in empty huts. Even children.

Mama felt sad whenever she thought of how those people must have suffered.

"They lost more than just their health, Mary-Margaret," she told me.

"What d'you mean?" I asked her.

"They lost hope for a better way of life."

I didn't really know what she meant until she explained what it must have been like to see so many people around you die.

"Imagine all your brothers and sisters dying from smallpox," she said, "Imagine Daddy and I dying, too. Imagine what it would be like to be all alone with none of your own people to help you."

I did imagine. And I cried. Because even just imagining it made me frightened. It would be hard to hope for better things if there was just you doing all the hoping, I thought.

Somebody must have hoped for them because they did survive. But it was a long time before they could forget the terror of smallpox and look forward to happier times.

Another epidemic broke out in 1918 which was also frightening. It was the Spanish 'flu and everyone got sick from it.

It started in Europe where the First World War was being fought. In fact, 1918 was the year the war ended. As the soldiers returned to their homes in Canada and the United States, they brought the 'flu with them.

By the fall of 1918, people were starting to get scared, especially when they read this report on October 3 in the "Colonist" newspaper:

"Further spread of Spanish influenza over the country and in army camps, with an increasing death rate, was indicated today in reports received by the public health service and at the office of the Surgeon-General of the army. New cases. . .totalled 12,004."

Then, when 5 people got sick with 'flu in Vancouver, Mayor Gale suggested that children should be stopped from going to theatres and movie houses.

Of course, none of us liked that at all but when the

Hastings Street is named after Admiral George Fowler Hastings who was the Commander-in-Chief of the Pacific Naval Station.

Richards Street is named after Cptn. George Richards who surveyed most of the British Columbia coastline in the early 1860s.

Davie Street is named after Alexander Edmund Batson Davie, premier of B.C. from 1887 to 1889. He was a lawyer and entered the B.C. Bar in 1873. His poor health forced him to resign his premiership and he died on August 1, 1889, at the age of 43.

Main Street was first named Westminster Avenue, which was originally known as False Creek Trail. Westminster Avenue became Main Street in 1910 when the city passed a bylaw authorizing the name change.

Georgia Street is named after King George III whom Captain George Vancouver had honoured in 1792 when he had named the waters between the mainland and Vancouver Island as the Gulf of Georgia.

Denman Street is named after Denman Island which was named by Captain Richards after Rear Admiral Joseph Denman, commander-in-chief of the Pacific Station from 1864 to 1866.

epidemic really hit Vancouver, Victoria, and the Fraser Valley; all the public places—churches, theatres, pool rooms, movie houses, and schools—were closed. Then we realized how serious the sickness was.

By October 15, there were 300 people sick in Vancouver with 'flu. Two days later, there were 500 sick and King Edward High School was converted into a hospital.

Within days, the whole city was shut down! Marriages were put off. Funerals were held outside because nobody was allowed to gather in a confined place as a group. Stores were disinfected every day. Lots of people started buying cinnamon, especially in Victoria where there were even more sick people, because they believed it was an antidote to the 'flu.

One night, Daddy came home exhausted. He had walked all the way home from work. He had avoided taking the streetcar so that he wouldn't catch the virus.

"I've never seen the city so deserted," he said as Mama put a plate of hot beef stew in front of him and ladled potatoes on top.

"All the department stores and markets will be shut down this Saturday," she told him.

At that moment, I was reading a book. Suddenly I heard the ladle crash onto Daddy's plate. I looked up. There was Mama bending over Daddy using her apron to try to stop his nose bleeding.

I was struck dumb with horror. What was happening. . .? What was the matter with Daddy. . .?

I looked at Mama's terrified face. That's when I knew. Daddy had the dreaded 'flu!

Vancouver's Park

Vancouver City Archives.

"Trotski" was a brown bear from Siberia. He was presented to the Stanley Park Zoo in 1919 but died a short time after.

The first animal exhibited in Stanley Park was a black bear chained to a tree stump. The park keeper was a man called Mr. Avison and his son, Henry, remembers what happened one day to make people wonder if that was the best place to keep a bear.

"...a minister's wife poked the old bear with her umbrella. The bear tore her umbrella and all of her skirt off."

As a result, a bear pit was dug and bears were put on display in there. By 1889, a number of caged animals were on display too. In 1901, an elk paddock was built, and in 1905, a deer paddock was constructed. In 1909, grey squirrels were brought in from the New York Park Department. The first animals obtained from a foreign zoo were black swans. They were obtained in 1901 from New South Wales Zoological Society Zoological Gardens in Australia.

Up until then, the exhibits had been spread over the park area. In 1915, the site for the present-day zoo was established and the exhibits moved to their new quarters. In 1947, the first miniature train was introduced and was a smash hit. It clacked around a

Stanley Zoo

Tickets, please! A ride on the miniature railway at the Children's Zoo in Stanley Park.

circuit where the modern Children's Zoo (built in 1963) now stands.

The Miniature Railway moved to its present location because of a rare and spectacular natural event—Hurricane Frieda. In 1962, this violent hurricane ravaged through Stanley Park, uprooting and smashing thousands of trees. The storm was so bad that winds peaked at almost 140 kph.

Park officials decided to make good use of the cleared areas, and in 1964, the new Miniature Railway went into operation in its present location.

The train has 3 engines. Two of them are called "Change" engines but the third is the most special. It is an exact, scaled-down replica of C.P.R. Engine 374, the first to make the transcontinental trip to Vancouver in 1887.

The Children's Zoo is the petting zoo where children can fondle the free-roaming animals—goats, llamas, donkeys, cows, sheep, and many others.

The zoo is not only a place to entertain and teach children about animals. Sometimes it is a temporary home for wild animals that have wandered into the city or become stranded on the beach.

Fun in the park!

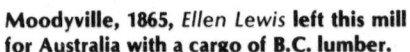

Moodyville, 1865, *Ellen Lewis* **left this mill for Australia with a cargo of B.C. lumber.**

I helped Mama get him into bed. He was sweating and shivering all at once and he was so dizzy he kept falling over as we guided him into the bedroom. He kept saying words that we couldn't understand and his nose wouldn't stop bleeding.

I don't remember much of that night. It was the most terrifying of my life.

Daddy was sick for 10 days. He never remembered much of those days and he nearly died.

How Mama worked, trying to save Daddy. The doctor gave her a prescription for some whiskey. You couldn't buy liquor then because of the prohibition laws that stopped the sale of liquor. You had to have a doctor's prescription to buy it. Mama joined the long lineup outside the liquor store and bought the best bottle of whiskey she could find.

I don't know if that was what cured Daddy but he got better anyway. That was when Mama got sick and she had to have whiskey, too.

It was an exhausting and frightening time but somehow we got through it.

Epidemics weren't the only disasters we faced when Vancouver was growing up. There were floods. Not from rains but from the swelling rivers during the spring melt in the mountains.

The first terrible flood happened in 1894 when, after a hard winter with lots of snow, the spring runoff was heavier than usual. The Fraser River rose and rose and rose. Bridges and dykes were washed away and the entire Fraser Valley looked like one gigantic lake.

Crops and livestock were washed away and even

little children drowned when they fell into the water. Not even the trains could get through. One man, who made his way across the valley on a raft, said that all he could see anywhere was water with just the roofs of houses cutting through the surface and the bodies of horses and cattle floating all around.

"There was this wee little bit of a girl," the man told us later when he visited Daddy. Mama told me later he was a work friend of Daddy's. "She couldn't have been more than 9 years old. She was all alone in a row boat, huggin' her pet lamb to herself to stop the crazy thing from jumping into the water. I dunno how she wasn't hauled into the water herself by that blinking animal!"

I stared at him, picturing what it must have been like for the girl trying so hard to save her pet. I shivered. I hadn't thought of the flood in terms of saving pets and being alone. Mama must have seen me shiver.

"Go put the pot on for tea, Mary-Margaret," she said firmly, her eyes ordering me out of the room. But I didn't want to go. I wanted to hear more. But, when I listened at the door, I wished I hadn't.

"I came across another boat too," Daddy's friend went on, "It wasn't such a pretty sight. The whole fam'ly dead. Mother. Father. Three littl' uns. Someone must've found them before me. They were all tied together...."

Outside the door, I shuddered, squeezing my eyes shut trying not to picture a whole family dead and

A typical homestead in Surrey.

The Fraser River from Fort Langley in 1860.
Painted by James M. Alden.

In 1827, the Hudson's Bay Company established Fort Langley on the Fraser River. Here, Indians traded furs for hatchets, knives, muzzle-loading guns, powder, matches, and blankets.

bundled together like...I could only think of firewood and that was when I started to cry. Mama heard me and, as I tried to make tea for her, Daddy, and their friend, I felt her arm around my shoulders.

"They're at peace now."

It was all she said and I hoped she was right.

It was another 54 years before a flood hit the valley again. It was 1948, just after the end of the Second World War. The flood was as bad, if not worse, than the one of 1894, and after it, a whole system of dykes, bigger and stronger than before, was built to control floods in the future.

The most difficult time that affected us as a family was the Great Depression. It started in 1929 and lasted nearly 10 years, until 1939.

Like all disasters, it happened suddenly. But, this time, it happened far away. In New York.

The 1920s had been good years, Daddy said, and lots of people who wouldn't normally buy stock at the Stock Exchange now had some savings with which they could afford to invest in companies.

"Stock" is money raised by a company from the sale of units called "shares." People buy these shares at the Stock Exchange and the company uses the money to develop a product. Later, when the product is sold and makes a profit, the shareholders, the people who bought the shares, have a share of the profit.

In 1929, all kinds of people began buying stock. This forced the price of stock up. People then made profits by buying and selling stock because the price of it was going up so quickly.

Kitchen scale.

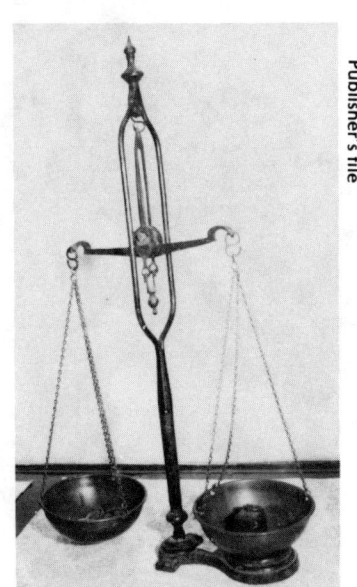

Balance scale.

Then, in September, people stopped buying stock and, instead, sold it and kept the money. As the prices went down faster and faster, more and more people panicked and sold their stock. Lots of people lost money because they sold their stock for less than they had paid.

The worst day was October 29, 1929, when so many people were selling their stock that it became known as the heaviest day of trading in the history of the New York Stock Exchange.

Across the continent, the same thing was happening at the Vancouver Stock Exchange. Even the safest, most reliable stock was suddenly only worth half its value.

Suddenly, businesses everywhere stopped working. The building industry was one of the first. Because Daddy was a carpenter, he was one of the first to lose his job.

By the end of the year there were lineups of people waiting for food outside the city relief offices right across the country. There were no jobs. No income. No food. No clothes. No car to run because no one could afford the gas.

People begged, borrowed or stole whatever they could to get by. Single men grouped together in shacks and hovels. They were made from old lumber and they were called "jungles." The men begged for food. They searched endlessly for jobs. They were nearly always sick from one disease or another because they couldn't look after themselves properly.

The Depression was horrible on children. So many

The year of Vancouver's first Depression was 1893. Unemployment was high, churches set up soup kitchens, and railways went broke.

Photos courtesy Vancouver Aquarium

The Vancouver Aquarium

One of the most famous and well-loved places in Vancouver is the Vancouver Aquarium.

The Aquarium opened on July 15, 1956. It was designed to accommodate 100,000 visitors and there was a staff of 6 people with Mr. Murray Newman as curator. The aquarium was so popular that, within a year, visitors totalled 400,000. Almost as soon as it opened, the aquarium needed to expand.

Over the years, it did expand. One of the most dramatic additions was the Graham Amazon Gallery opened by Her Majesty Queen Elizabeth II on March 9, 1983. It features the plants of the Amazon jungle. It houses exotic birds, a lazy sloth, turtle-filled rock pools, iguanas, and the sights and recorded sounds of a tropical rainforest.

The latest expansion is the new whale habitat for the aquarium's 3 prized killer whales, Hyak, Finna, and Bjossa. What is so special about having a "whale habitat" as opposed to just having a "whale pool" is that the habitat consists of several pools. Whales can enjoy their own space. If one of them wants to be alone, he can go into another pool, rather like you going into another room at home if you want to be by yourself.

As much as the aquarium is a place of entertainment, it is also a place of learning. Research is a full-time activity at the aquarium and its biologists share their findings with visiting school children through the aquarium's education program.

The Vancouver Aquarium, like the Stanley Park Zoo, is a member of the American Association of Zoological Parks and Aquariums (AAZPA). Not only do member zoos and aquariums share their research findings and experiences with each other, they share their animals too.

They loan each other animals for breeding purposes or for exhibit. Whenever they can, they trade animals with each other. Through the "Species Survival Plan," they encourage the breeding of rare and endangered animals. By breeding captive stocks of rare animals, zoos and aquariums are preventing sub-species of animals from becoming extinct.

A lot of people question whether it is fair to keep animals in captivity.

These days, it is necessary for wild lands to be controlled and managed. This means managing the wild animals too. But you have to know HOW to manage them. Only by watching animals in the wild and studying them intensely in captivity can you find out all the information you need to properly manage and protect them.

That is the role of zoos and aquariums. Helping children understand this role is one of Vancouver Aquarium's most important goals.

The greatest diameter of a Douglas fir tree on record is 7 metres. This giant tree grew in southern Vancouver Island. When it fell because of butt-rot on November 29, 1913, local residents thought it was an earthquake. The tree was estimated to be 1,500 years old. It would have started growing when the Roman Empire was about to crumble.

The second greatest recorded diameter of a Douglas fir is 5 metres. This tree was felled in 1886 at the corner of Granville and Georgia Streets in Vancouver.

The Douglas fir, one of British Columbia's most important commercial trees, is the world's third largest species of tree.

of them were starving. They only had rags for clothes and most of them didn't have any shoes at all. Older children stayed in school longer during the Depression because there weren't any jobs to leave school for.

The city and the government tried to give relief to families but it was not nearly enough. In 1932, $9 was given to each head of a family each month, $3.50 for a second adult, and $2.50 for each child. I can remember Mama trying desperately to spread the relief payments through the month and feed all of us.

Of course, food was cheap to buy then because of the Depression. You could get 12 kilograms of potatoes for 15¢ and 2 dozen oranges for 25¢. You could buy coffee and 2 donuts at a coffee shop for 5¢ and have bacon and eggs for 15¢.

Things did get better though. But it took years. By the time the Depression was over another sad chapter in history was about to start: The Second World War.

It wasn't until after the war when life became prosperous and happy again that the final memories of the Great Depression were gone. By that time, everyone was throwing their energies into what Mama called the "post-war boom years" and life was for living and working at again. . . .

You can see how big the Douglas fir trees were compared to John and me!

To feed all its animals, the Vancouver Aquarium has to buy 75 tonnes of food every year.

Highlights of 100 years of Policing

1895   First incidence of safe cracking reported.
1904   Policemen first issued with flashlights for night patrol.
1907   The "Fixed Point System" was set up in which each constable was assigned a "point" within the city and had to stand there for his entire shift so that, when a citizen wanted a police constable, he or she would know where to find one.

Three bicycles were bought for the patrol sergeants so that they could visit their men at their points and, in the same year, the first paddy wagon was bought. A paddy wagon is a locked vehicle you put prisoners in to take them to jail.
1908   The first finger prints were taken by Vancouver Police Department.
1909   Curfew bylaw in which children under 16 had to be off the city streets by 9:00 p.m.

First mounted patrolman in Stanley Park.
1910   The Siege of Deadman's Island. The police occupied the island for more than a year to prevent it from being logged.
1911   First motorcycle purchased for use by the Detective Division.
1914   The Police Pipe Band organized with 20 members.
1922   The rule of the road changed from driving on the left to driving on the right hand side. The Traffic Division was formed.
1925   "Prowler Car System" introduced to try to fight crime.
1935   School Patrol set up.
1938   First Training School set up for policemen.
1954   New Police and Court Building constructed at 312 Main Street.
1957   Dog Squad established with 3 dogs (Jiggs, Sam, and King) and 3 masters.

The Carey Fir Legend

Atop the Carey fir!

If legend is fact, then the tallest tree of all time was a Douglas fir that stood in Lynn Valley in North Vancouver in the 1890s.

It was said to have been 129 metres high. (The tallest tree known today is a coast redwood 119 metres high standing in Redwood Creek Valley in northern California.)

The Lynn Valley fir was cut by George Carey. He claimed the tree was 92 metres high to the first limb and that it was 8 metres in diameter.

Over the years, many foresters have doubted that such a tree ever existed but historians have found that the records on the Carey fir are so consistent in detail that the tree cannot be discredited.

In his later years, George Carey denied the statistics of the tree. But lovers of legends believe that Carey had been influenced by skeptical loggers who made him doubt his own figures.

Today, all trace of the tree is gone. We'll never know for sure if it existed but, if it did, then the forests of Vancouver can claim that it would have been the tallest living thing ever recorded in all of Earth's history....

Vancouver Police Station and car, 1907.

5. Protecting Vancouver

There were policemen in Vancouver before it became a city. As far back as 1871, people were worried about a need for law and order. Originally, keeping the peace had been handled by a government agent called Tomkins Brew but, when he didn't keep the peace very well, a man called Jonathan Miller was appointed as constable.

Mr. Miller lived in a cottage which he also used as his courthouse and jail. In 1883, his work was helped by a man called John Stewart who was hired as a watchman to prowl the streets at night and watch the stores.

When Vancouver became a city in 1886, the first council meeting was held in Mr. Miller's cottage. They wanted to appoint a police chief. Everyone wanted Mr. Miller to be the chief but he had already decided that he wanted the job of postmaster. The mayor wanted John Stewart, the night watchman, but the magistrate wanted a man called Mr. Johnson.

The city's fathers say...

"Not more than 25 cows shall be kept by any one person, family, partnership, company or corporation at any one time within the...limits of the city."
Bylaw Number 263, 16 January 1902

"No person shall bathe or swim in the waters of Burrard Inlet or English Bay within the City limits between the hours of 6:00 in the forenoon and 8:00 in the evening without a bathing dress covering the body from the neck to the knees, and any person wearing such proper bathing dress may bathe at any time in the waters of Burrard Inlet or English Bay within the City limits."
Bylaw Number 135, 17 March 1892

"Old people say Indians see first white man up near Squamish. When they see first ship they think it an island with 3 dead trees...."
August Jack Khahtsahlano

The first Canadian aircraft engine was tested by its designer, W. W. Gibson, in a twin plane. The test was carried out near Victoria on September 8, 1910. The first plane to fly near Vancouver was a Curtiss pusher biplane piloted by Charles Hamilton on March 25, 1910.

It was the city clerk who had the job of casting the deciding vote. At the time, he was dating Mr. Stewart's daughter so you can guess who he voted for. John Stewart!

The next person appointed was a jailer and the man who spent the most time in jail was John Clough. Daddy said he spent so much time in jail for drunkenness he might as well be in charge.

But, do you know, it was Mr. Clough who was a hero after the great fire. He found blankets for the survivors. Of course, nobody realized that he had been stealing the blankets from the jail and hiding them in the forest nearby.

After the fire, 3 more constables were sworn in to keep law and order, which was becoming a very hard job. All kinds of bad people were coming to Vancouver. When the City Hall was still housed in a tent after the fire, one of these characters stuffed a human leg in a boot and hung it outside the tent. Can you imagine? The place got to be known as "Leg and Boot Square."

The first building owned by the city after the great fire was the new police and court building erected in the 100 block on East Powell Street. It was also used as a city hall, as a Sunday school, and for concerts.

Even back then, drugs were a problem in Vancouver. In 1887, there were 50 opium addicts. Opium, which was brought in from the Orient, was a legal drug then and you could buy it from distributors in the city.

In 1907, the Dominion government sent a young

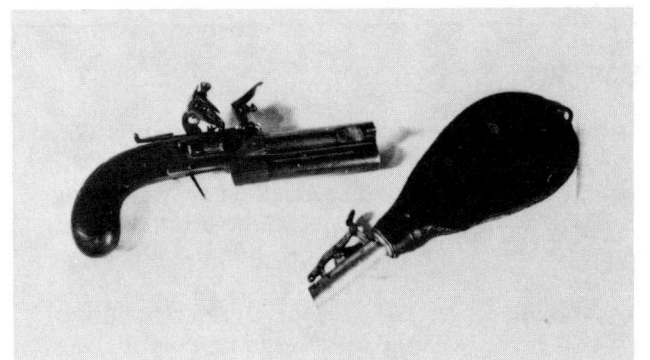

5) I spy with my little eye
a square in the middle of town
named after a tree
and watched constantly
by a man who sailed here
with his hound.

politician called MacKenzie King to investigate the race riots. He found out how popular opium was. After he went back to Ottawa and reported its use, the first narcotic prohibition legislation was introduced. MacKenzie King became Prime Minister for Canada in 1921.

There were chain gangs in the late 1800s—groups of prisoners chained together to do labour. The first man sentenced to the chain gang in Vancouver was a cook off a ship. He was caught stealing laundry from clothes lines.

The first policewomen in Vancouver were Laurancy Harris and Minnie Miller. They joined the police force in 1912 to help the young girls and women in the city, Mama said.

In 1921, there were 4 policewomen and one of them, a Miss E. LeSueur, was fired almost as soon as she was hired. You see, she was an active member of the "Woman's Pioneer Political Equality League" which was frowned on by the men. Because she was involved in the women's liberation movement, she was dismissed.

Her activities made the police chief nervous about having women on the police force for many years. He hired only widows and policemen. But women still joined the police force anyway because, by 1948, there were 15 policewomen working in the patrol cars and riding in the Mounted Squad.

The 1930s were very hard years for lots of people. There were very few jobs so lots of people were unemployed. The members of the Vancouver Police

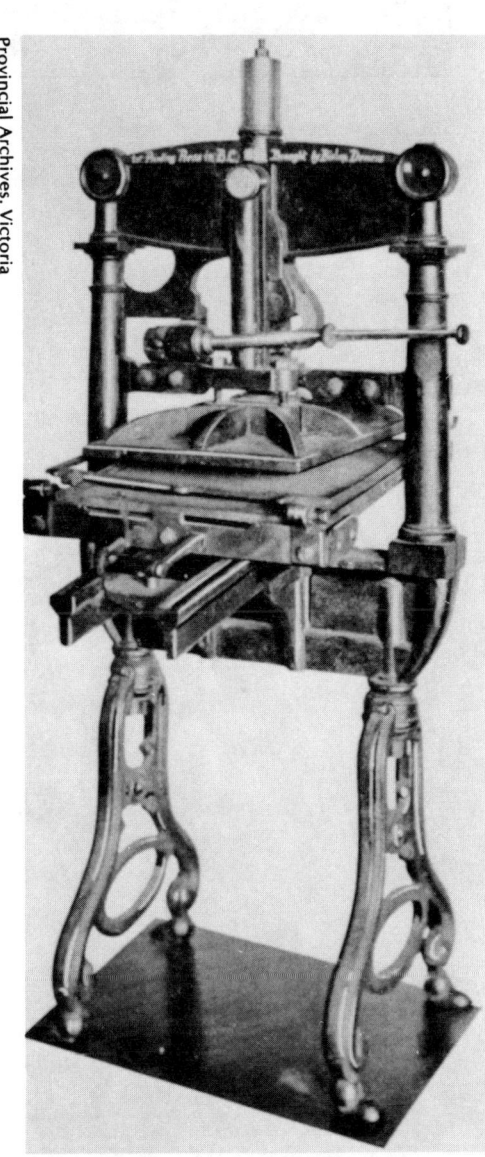

Provincial Archives, Victoria

Demers Printing press. The first printing press in B.C.

The first printing press was brought to British Columbia from France in 1856 by Bishop Demers. It was used by Count Paul de Carro.

DOGS IN POLICE WORK

The first recorded instance of the use of dogs in police work was in St. Malo, France, in the early part of the 14th century when they were used to guard dock installations. The use of dogs continued until 1770 when the practice stopped after a young naval officer was killed by one of the dogs.

Dogs were used in Paris in 1895 to combat street gangs. The German police force began using them in 1896. The Germans experimented in breeding, training, and how to use the dogs. The Germans chose the German Shepherd as the best breed of dog for police work because of its intelligence and adaptability.

The first school set up to train dogs for police work was established in Greenheide, Germany in 1920. The dogs were trained in basic obedience, tracking, and searching. This school laid the foundation for modern police dog training.

Today, the German Shepherd is used by law enforcement agencies around the world and is the only breed used by the Vancouver Police Department.

Department tried to help them. On November 23, 1930, they opened the "Blue Coat Inn." By December 31, 1930, they had given away: 4,929 meals, 33 pairs of underwear, 17 pairs of pants, 84 pairs of socks, and 71 pairs of shoes and had repaired 38 pairs of boots.

But, despite their help, life was still difficult. Many people looked to the city and the government for help but, in 1938, Mayor Miller discontinued relief for unemployed people.

As a result, people started begging on street corners with tin cans. That's why it was called "tin-canning." A bylaw was passed to make it illegal, but people went on begging anyway. There were sit-ins and protests and even a riot. The police had such a hard time keeping order that one constable lost his revolver. After that, the policemen were allowed to wear their revolvers in Sam Brown holsters outside their tunics instead of in special pockets under their tunics.

Did you know that the Vancouver Police Department was the first municipal force in Canada to start a dog squad? It was set up in 1957 and the first dogs—all German Shepherds—were called Jiggs, Sam, and King.

All the Vancouver Police Dogs are trained to: (1) be obedient; (2) be steady under gunfire and attack if they have to; (3) guard a prisoner and stop his (or her) escape; (4) face noisy crowds and rioting people; (5) search buildings or areas for criminals; (6) chase a running suspect and stop him or her; (7) attack; (8) track; (9) search for objects that might be evidence of a crime; (10) work by himself if his master is attacked or injured.

Protecting the people of Vancouver means having a hospital as well as a police force.

Like the city hall, the first hospital was a tent! You see, after the great fire when the city was being rebuilt, the Canadian Pacific Railway track was being built from Port Moody to Vancouver. A hospital was set up in a tent by the side of the track where injured railway workers were looked after.

But, of course, that wasn't good enough to care for sick people. I can remember how Mama and Daddy were always saying we needed a proper building for something as important as a hospital. Everybody else said the same thing, too.

This is why there was a wooden building put up quickly on a lot just north of Powell Street between Hawkes and Heatley Avenues. All it could hold was 9 beds and it was always crowded.

In September, 1886, the Board of Health, with the agreement of the C.P.R. took over running the building and it became the first city hospital.

Two years later, the hospital moved to a two-storey building on Beatty Street. It had 35 beds. In the 1890s, 2 red brick additions were built on so that, by 1902, the city hospital could look after 50 patients.

But the hospital still needed more space. In January, 1902, the city bought about 2.2 hectares of land on the Fairview Ridge, overlooking False Creek, from

Fairview buildings in the shadow of Vancouver General Hospital, 1915.

A horse-drawn ambulance.

"...If a child is thin, let him take a little of Scott's emulsion of cod-liver oil."

the Canadian Pacific Railway. It cost them $5,500. In June, 1902, the Vancouver General Hospital was incorporated by a special act of the Legislature, and soon after that, building started on the new hospital that would, one day, be one of the biggest in Canada.

But, back then, nobody would have believed that! Why, there were even letters to the newspaper saying how terrible it was to build the hospital way out there in the forest! You see, 10th Avenue south of False Creek, where the hospital stands today, didn't even exist then. It was still wilderness and access to the new hospital site was across a plank bridge that spanned the creek and then along a dirt trail to the building site.

Daddy used to do the journey every morning. He was one of the carpenters who laid the first beam on the hospital and he still remembers how everyone grumbled about its forest location.

The ground for the hospital had been prepared by a man called Hector Girvan. Daddy always remembered him because of his dog, Sport. You see, every morning Mr. Girvan left home at about 5:00 a.m. with a team of horses to clear the land of trees, pull out the stumps, and plough and level the ground to get it ready for building.

Every morning, Sport would walk between the 2 horses on the way to work. You know why? There were always yappy dogs who would bark at the team on the way. So Sport would walk between the horses, watching for the yappy mongrels. If one so much as DARED to start barking, he would run up to it, grab it by the scruff of

Victorian Order of Nurses.

its neck, and dump it on the side of the trail!

Daddy used to call Sport Mr. Girvan's official "Yapper-Remover."

Building the new hospital started in October, 1902, but it wasn't ready for patients until 1906 when horse-drawn ambulances took the first 47 patients to the new site.

Sick people with infectious diseases didn't go there, though. At first, they were left in the old hospital building. Then, later, cottages for infectious diseases were built at the new site. A high wooden fence was built around them and relatives and friends did their visiting through the slats and knot holes at a safe distance.

People who had tuberculosis were even more of a problem. The nurses didn't want them brought into the hospital in case everyone got tuberculosis. They had to stay in tents put up on the grounds.

It wasn't fun being sick, back then.

Visitor parking was a problem, even then. A horse shed had to be built for carriage horses. The doctors helped with money toward the cost of that. A shed was also built for 3 cows but, instead, it became a chicken coop.

When the First World War broke out in 1914, the people who ran the hospital realized they would have to have a special military area for wounded servicemen. A military annex opened June 10, 1917, and by October, 1919, more than 10,000 servicemen had been cared for there.

Polio was a frightening sickness in the years after the war. Between 1945 and 1955, there were 573 cases of it. When the Salk vaccine was introduced in 1955 to protect children from polio, there was a dramatic decrease in the outbreak of the disease. By 1956, only 8 cases had been reported in Vancouver.

Bedpan

In January 1951, Vancouver sampled its first commercial frozen apple juice concentrate made by B.C. Fruit Processors Ltd.

Medicine chest of Dr. John Helmcken

The hospital was always full, but one of the worst years was 1918 when there was an epidemic of Spanish 'flu. So many people were sick that the hospital was overflowing with patients and some had to be cared for in schools, churches, and halls.

Health care then wasn't like it is today. There weren't any shots or immunization programs. People would get sick from smallpox or diphtheria, and every year, babies died from what Mama called summer complaint.

"What's that?" I asked her once. Earlier that day I had seen this tiny white casket being taken out of a house. The door had a black banner on it and the mother and father wore black armbands. I remember how they cried, following that little white casket, and I had wanted to cry too.

Mama told me that summer complaint was caused by bad milk. You see, back then, milk wasn't pasteurized or refrigerated. It was delivered by the milkman who brought it on a wagon in 2 big milk cans balanced on the back. The measuring cup hung on the side where the dust would stick to it and the flies would buzz around it all the time. When he delivered your milk to you, he would tip the big milk can and pour some milk into the measuring cup which, of course, was full of germs from the dust and the flies. But we didn't know that then.

One time, Mama had a clear glass jug which she put the milk into. She was staring at this jug and I couldn't think why until she held it up to show Daddy.

"Look," she said, and pointed to a thick layer of dirt at the bottom of the jug.

> **VANCOUVER GENERAL HOSPITAL**
> **1906 Statistics**
>
> Six months after the great fire of 1886, a man called Dr. A. M. Robertson arrived in Vancouver. He wrote about the little hospital that had been built at the east end of Powell Street.
>
> "There were only 5 or 6 beds under the care of a man and his wife," he wrote, "and it served for the reception of Canadian Pacific Railway surgical and medical cases. It became part of my daily routine to plough my way through the mud out to this so-called hospital. It was kept pretty busy and a lot of good work was done, in spite of the almost total lack of nursing..."
>
> Population of Vancouver: 50,000
>
> By the year's end, 104 patients were being actively cared for. They comprised 71 men and 33 women. A total of 1,313 patients had been admitted to the hospital and 25 births had taken place. In 1906, the hospital staff included: a hospital superintendent; a matron; a dispenser; a housekeeper; an engineer; a nursing superintendent; 2 assistant superintendents; a dietitian; an operating room superintendent; 31 nursing students, and 4 probationers.
>
> The first nurse in the frontier area of what would later be Vancouver was Emily Susan Branscombe Peabody Patterson. She arrived in 1872 with her husband, John, who became a master stevedore at Hastings Mill.
>
> The first matron in the new city hospital was Mrs. Roberts. She had been trained in hospital management and nursing care in London, England.
>
> When Mrs. Roberts left the hospital, Miss Crickmay took her place at a monthly salary of $40. She wrote, "The patients were mostly a rather tough lot of men, the type that flock to frontier towns. Nursing them was no pleasant task."

Daddy stared at it. He was horrified. Then he had an idea. "Boil it, Grace," he said, "That'll get rid of that dirt."

"Boil it?" she asked him and she raised her eyebrows the way she does when she doesn't understand things.

He nodded firmly, so that's what Mama did. What she was doing, of course, was pasteurizing the milk but she didn't realize that. Because we sterilized our milk this way, nobody in our house got summer complaint. Much later on, I found out that summer complaint was called "dysentery."

Daddy said it was a real turning point in our society when the health people realized that flies carried germs. We didn't have screen doors and lots of homes still used outhouses as toilets. There were flies between the kitchen and the outhouse all the time and they'd land on ANYTHING edible. No wonder people ended up running to the hospital instead of just to the outhouse!

Over the decades, the hospital got bigger and bigger and more and more specialized as new departments and research institutes and centres opened. Today, it is one of the most important hospitals in Canada.

Protecting Vancouver also meant having a fire department.

When Vancouver was born in April, 1886, there was already a tiny fire department which was run by the men at Hasting's Mill. But, the town site itself didn't have one. Of course, that was no good, so on May 28, there was a meeting at George Schletsky's clothing store to organize what was called the "Volunteer Hose Company No. 1." By June 2, the whole fire brigade had been organized and Sam Pedgriff had been elected chief.

But, the trouble was, the fire brigade didn't have a fire engine.

They were still trying to decide what to do about this when the great fire broke out on June 13 and almost wiped out the whole town. Well, you can imagine how badly the aldermen in the city council felt after THAT. They didn't waste any more time arguing about the cost of a fire engine.

An order was sent to the John D. Ronald Company of Brussels, Ontario, for a fire engine, 4 hose reels, and 770 metres of hose together with a cheque for $6,905. It arrived on July 26 at Port Moody.

A four-horse team pulled it nearly 20 kilometres over dusty roads to Vancouver and EVERYBODY in the whole town went out to meet it! Fire engines back then were known as steam pumps and this one was the greasiest, dustiest looking steamer anyone had ever seen. But, once all the dirt had been cleaned away, it was the shiniest thing I'd ever seen!

The city didn't have a horse team for the steamer

FIRE!

The coming of television brought hard times to movie theatres: within 18 months, 216 theatres had closed in Canada, 24 of them in B.C.

then. Whenever a fire broke out, the steam pump had to be pulled to the scene by the firemen. Sometimes, by the time they got there, the fire was almost over but they did manage to save a lot of houses and offices from flying sparks.

When Mr. John Howe Carlisle became fire chief in the fall of 1886, he made sure that he always knew what the latest developments were in fire fighting.

In May, 1887, he convinced city council to buy a hook and ladder truck. Then, in the fall, he convinced them that if they had a team of horses to pull the steamer, the fire brigade would get to fires faster. So they bought that too.

I can still remember the first time I saw a horse-drawn steamer racing to a fire. What a SIGHT! It was in winter, almost Christmas time, and it was dark. All day it had been snowing and the snow had turned to slush in the streets. Mama and I had gone shopping on Granville Street and we were just about to go home when we heard this great commotion. People were shouting, a team of horses was galloping down the middle of the street pulling the steam pump, and giant sparks were flying everywhere from their hooves and from the steamer's boiler. I have never SEEN such excitement as the fire brigade raced by. I had never seen such HUGE horses! What wonderful creatures they were and how brave as they tore through the slippery, dark streets, now shying for a moment from the roar of the people around them.

The firemen loved their animals. They must have loved wild animals too because, in the early 1900s, they used to keep a pet bear on a chain at the fire hall on the corner of Broadway and Granville. It was a small black bear and we used to pass it every day on our way to school. The Mamas and Daddies, though, didn't think that that was such a good idea. They never trusted the bear and, eventually, he was taken away.

A Great City

Before Vancouver was called Vancouver, it was known as Granville.

But a lot of people felt that the growing town should have a more important name.

When it was decided that Granville would be the site of the new railroad terminal, the residents went to the provincial government to incorporate it under a new name.

But what was it going to be called?

The same man who chose the site of the railroad terminal chose the name for the town: Mr. Van Horne.

"This is destined to be a GREAT city!" he exclaimed, "Perhaps the greatest in Canada. We must see to it that it has a name commensurate with its dignity and importance and Vancouver it shall be, if I have the ultimate decision."

He did. On April 6, 1886, Granville became the City of Vancouver.

Being a fireman meant you had to be fit. One of Daddy's brothers was a fireman with the Vancouver Hose Company and he was one of the 15 men who entered the Hose Competition at Tacoma, Washington, in 1889. The Vancouver team became the North American Hose Team Champions by defeating 12 American teams that year and, when they got home, each one of them was presented with a civic gold medal. Uncle still has it.

Every year the fire department added new equipment and machinery, and when motorized fire engines were first built, Chief Carlisle wanted those, too. So, in 1907, three Seagrave hosewagons arrived and, in 1908, the self-propelled steamer, called the *Amoskeag* was delivered.

Now that really was something. It had the biggest steam pump you ever saw and it could go about 20 kilometres per hour. It had great big wheels and each one was spiked to make its traction on the muddy roads better.

And, you know what, it was those spikes that caused utter chaos the first time the *Amoskeag* was called to a fire!

As soon as the bell hit, all the firemen clambered aboard and off they went. Well, everything was fine until

Loading ships at Moodyville, 1886.

Provincial Archives, Victoria

In 1871, the Colony of British Columbia joined the Dominion of Canada as a province. The Dominion promised the new province that a railroad to the Pacific would be built which would link the west coast with the eastern cities.

There was a lot of talk as to where the terminus of the railroad should be. The man who finally decided was the general manager of the Canadian Pacific Railway, Mr. William Cornelius Van Horne. He decided that the natural harbours on the south shore of Burrard Inlet were an ideal location for a seaport.

The land was cleared, track was laid linking the western provinces with the east, and on May 23, 1887, the first train arrived in Vancouver.

The spikes heaved up the wooden blocks and flung them all over the place...!

they went roaring down a road levelled with wooden blocks. The spikes lifted the wooden blocks and flung them all over the place! It was raining wooden blocks everywhere—on people, through store windows, onto the backs of skittery horses, onto yelping dogs and cats and the kids playing on the sidewalks. It was pandemonium and I don't know what did the most damage—the fire the steamer was racing to or the wooden blocks its wheels threw into the air . . . !

You can bet that, when they got back to the fire hall, the mechanics quickly took the spikes off.

During the 1920s, all the fire department apparatus was changed in colour from white to red and, in 1928, the city bought its first fireboat which was stationed at the No. 16 Fire Hall in False Creek.

By 1930, firemen were not only skilled at putting out fires but were learning first aid as well. Later on, the first aid service became the Rescue and Safety Branch. That was in 1942.

Have you ever thought what would happen if a fire

Publisher's file

NOTICE

Will teamsters and riders please refrain from hitching their horses to veranda posts, wagon wheels, and other breakable effects . . . . .

It took Mother Nature millions of years to create the land features where Vancouver would grow. The last stage of her "planning" happened when massive glaciers covered Canada during the Ice Age.

The Ice Age began about a million years ago and ended about 10,000 years ago. The glaciers of the Ice Age were so heavy that they pushed the level of the land down into the earth. When the climate warmed and the glaciers began to melt, the land rose up again and took the shape we know today as the coastal mountains, the Fraser Valley, and Burrard Inlet.

broke out and burned the telephone lines so you couldn't call for help?

That really happened once. On February 19, 1949, the administration building at Vancouver International Airport caught fire and the telephone lines were burned.

It was the radio operator in the Vancouver control tower who saved the day though. Do you know what he did? He radioed Calgary and Calgary tower turned in the first alarm to the Vancouver Fire Department! That call for help travelled nearly 2,000 kilometres round trip for a fire 8 kilometres from the fire hall!

During the 1950s, the fire department spent a lot of money replacing worn out equipment and buying as much up-to-date fire apparatus as they could.

Fireboat No. 2 was put into service in Vancouver Harbour and the first major fire it took part in was the fire that broke out in the United Grain Growers' wharf which did $1.5 million worth of damage!

The largest fire that happened though was the one at B.C. Forest Products. It happened on July 3, 1960, and it was the first five-alarm fire in the fire department's history. The first alarm came in at 5:26 p.m. when the captain of the fireboat, J. H. Carlisle, first noticed it. At its worst, the fire covered an area of 4 city blocks and it took over 350 fire fighters to battle the blaze. The fire did more than $3 million damage.

A MAMMOTH TALE OF DATING

In 1977, the bones of an American mastodon were dug up from a peat bog near Sequim, Washington, just 50 kilometres south of Victoria. A bone spearpoint was found in its ribs, proving the theory that mastodon meat was enjoyed by early Indians. A bison, killed and cut by hunting natives, was also found at the site. Scientists have calculated that the animals had been killed about 12,000 years ago.

How do we know how long ago a mammoth died or when a dinosaur lived?

Just after World War II, a man called Willard F. Libby developed a system of calculating when something died by measuring the amount of decay of radiocarbon (carbon-14) inside a specimen.

Most of the elements in nature are a mixture of several isotopes—atoms that are alike chemically but have different atomic weights. Some of these isotopes—carbon-14, uranium-234, chlorine-36 and others—are radio-active. They give off nuclear particles and decay into other elements. For example, carbon-14 decays into nitrogen-14.

Each isotope has its own rate of decay which is measured by its "half-life." This means, the amount of time it takes for half of the radioactive material to decay.

Carbon-14 is present in all living things. When an animal dies, the carbon-14 starts to decay. It takes 5,730 years for half of the carbon-14 to decay into nitrogen-14.

To calculate how long ago an animal died, scientists measure how much carbon-14 is left in the creature. Then they compare it to the isotope's "half-life."

This method of finding out how long ago a creature died is called Radiocarbon Dating. It is the most reliable method for specimens not older than 50,000 years and not younger than 500 years.

B.C. Lions vs. Calgary.

6. For the Sport of it all

Everybody loved sports. All it took was a ball and a couple of kids to get a game going at any time.

Sports were popular in school, too. There was an elementary school baseball league and schools used to play against each other. Sports days were, of course, the favourite day of school and there were the usual track and field events as well as Maypole dances, when children danced around a large pole holding colourful ribbons attached to the top.

We had house teams and the house that picked up the most points by winning most of the races was declared the winner of sports day.

There were all kinds of races—fast ones and slow ones. The funniest one was the slow bike race. I can remember the year John won it on his home-made bike.

The track was 45 metres long. The one who went the slowest won the race. You couldn't put your feet down so the only way you could steady yourself was to keep wobbling the handlebars.

B.C. Lions vs. Winnipeg — Kent Kallberg

B.C. Lions vs. Calgary — Photographer: Kent Kallberg

B.C. Lions vs. Montreal — Photographer: Jack Murray

How John WOBBLED! He seemed to be barely moving. And he was neck and neck with his best friend, Willie. Both of them tried to go slower and slower until I could swear they were almost backwards. But that's not allowed either!

It's funny, watching a race to be the SLOWEST. You're always cheering someone on to go the fastest but here was John trying to keep behind Willie—and Willie trying to keep behind John!

It ended up a tie. It was the race that took the longest to finish and the last thing they wanted to do was do it all over again to break the tie.

We decorated our bikes for sports day and some made a serious art out of decorating their bikes. John was one of those. He always took everything so seriously.

When I went to high school I joined the girls' grass hockey team. John was in soccer and football.

Grass hockey games were played every Saturday morning, no matter what the weather. I can remember one Saturday when it was SO foggy that, when we lined up in centre field for face-off, we couldn't see a THING.

"I can't see the goalie!" Suzie hissed to me as she raced down the field.

"I can't even see the ball!" I giggled back.

That was when I saw it coming straight for me. I cracked it wildly with my stick to stop it from hitting me and a second later I heard a voice yell, "GOAL!"

Suzie and I couldn't stop laughing. In fact, the rest of the game was just wild as we kept trying to see the goals, the goalies, the ball, and the players. It was one of the most hysterical games we've ever played.

Everyone loved hockey. The game was brought to Vancouver by the Patrick family who moved here in 1910 from Nelson, B.C.

In the early 1900s, Joseph Patrick was a successful businessman in the lumber industry. He had 2 sons, Frank and Lester, who spent their winters playing professional hockey in Brandon and Montreal.

When their father sold their lumber business, the family decided to start their own professional hockey league in the west.

In 1910 they moved to Vancouver. They built what would be the largest indoor ice rink in the world. It was called the Denman Arena and it opened in 1911. They built another rink in Victoria.

The sons recruited hockey players from the National Hockey Association and built up their teams with local players. In the 1914-15 season, the "Vancouver Millionaires," the name of the Patrick family's team, won the Stanley Cup against the Ottawa Senators. The game was played at the Denman Arena and it was THE sports event of the year.

It was a long time before there were other professional sports, which was a shame because Vancouver had always had a lot of sports fans.

When the glaciers of the Ice Age melted, bare land was uncovered and the howling wind blew great billows of dust.

This was not ordinary dust. It was a very special, silky kind of dust we call "loess" (pronounced "less"). The dust had been made by the glaciers.

As the glaciers had flowed across the land, they had scooped up trees, bushes, rocks, and boulders in their path. Inside the glaciers, where ice churns around like a gigantic grinding machine, the rocks and vegetation were pulverized into dust. Because the rocks and vegetation were full of minerals, the dust was too. When the glaciers melted and the dust was free to blow over the land, it settled to form the soil on which the great cedar and fir forests grow.

"Tiger" Williams getting a pat on the head from goaltender Richard Brodeur.

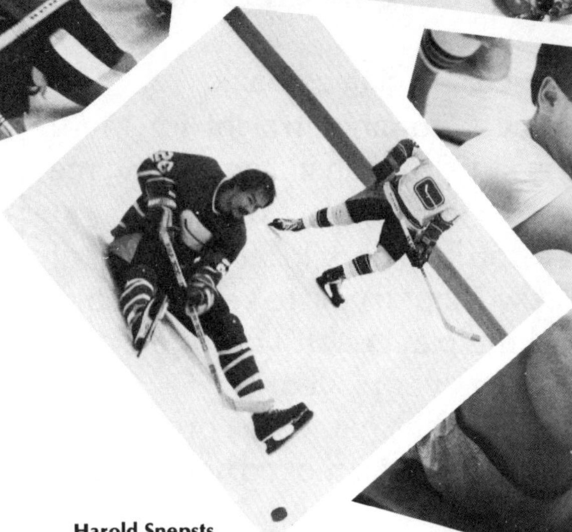

Where's the puck gone?

Harold Snepsts sitting this one out.

Stan Smyl— The agony of a warm-up!

Photos Courtesy Vancouver Canucks

The origins of hockey

Hockey is believed to be the oldest game in the world played with a stick and a ball.

It started in Persia (now Iran) around 2,000 B.C. The ancient Greeks and Romans played a stick and ball game and there is a picture of a "face-off" with 6 players on a wall built by Themistocles who was an Athenian politician. He lived in Athens between the years 524 and 460 B.C.

The Aztecs and the American Indians also played a stick game with a ball. In France in the Middle Ages the game was called "hoquet" French for "shepherd's crook."

When the British began playing the game, the word changed to "hockey."

Early telephones

Publisher's file

The first telephone installation on mainland B.C. was a line set up by the Rev. William Duncan in the Indian village of Metlakatla between the village store and the sawmill.

6) I spy with my little eye
stores all bunched in a mall
that's made just for kids
with a skill to get rid
of allowances—just for a ball!

The B.C. Lions played its first professional football game against the Winnipeg Blue Bombers on August 28, 1954. The team won its first Grey Cup in 1964. The game was played in Toronto and the Lions beat the Tiger-Cats in a 34-24 win.

Baseball didn't do as well in Vancouver as hockey and football. There was a professional baseball team in town from 1957 to 1969 but it had too many money problems to be successful.

By now, professional ice hockey was the number one sport of the country. The National Hockey League had been formed in 1917 with 5 Canadian teams. The first U.S. team joined in 1924. The league expanded and re-organized itself in 1967, and by 1970 consisted of 14 teams, including the Vancouver Canucks.

Vancouver had wanted to be a part of the league since it had begun to expand in the mid-1960s. While businessmen spent several years negotiating a franchise with the league, the Pacific Coliseum was built. It was finished in 1968. The franchise was bought for $6 million in 1969, and in 1970, the Canucks played their first NHL game against Los Angeles. They lost 3-1.

The Vancouver Whitecaps started playing professional soccer in 1974 but the team broke up 10 years later. People love soccer, though, and there is a good possibility that a professional team will return to Vancouver.

Vancouver is full of all kinds of amateur sports activities—cricket, cycling, fencing, billiards, curling, golf, horseback riding, racquetball, sailing, skiing, skating, swimming, volleyball, and lots more.

Families loved to play sports too, even if it was only batting a ball or racing around the city park.

Daddy always said team sports brought out the strong character in people. They learned to play and share the skill of the game together. They learned to share the triumph of winning and the lessons of losing.

And, Daddy said, what people learned from sports would help them play the biggest sport of all. Life.

The first man to trade in telephones was a Mr. Robert McMicking who, in 1878, became an agent for the Bell Telephone Co. in B.C. He set up a telephone line between the Telegraph Office in Victoria and the Colonist newspaper.

Royal Hudson

The Royal Hudson Number 2860

The first Canadian Pacific Hudson-type locomotives were built in 1929 by Montreal Locomotive Works. They were named after the Hudson River and were thought to be among the most handsome of engines with their distinctive streamlining, and elegant Tuscan red and black C.P.R colours.

The Hudsons could be identified by their 4-6-4 wheel arrangement and they had a larger firebox than earlier locomotives which produced more superheated steam at a higher boiler pressure. This meant that they could move faster and pull heavier trains than earlier engines.

In 1939, Hudson 2850 pulled the Royal Tour train which took King George VI and Queen Elizabeth, now the Queen Mother, on a 3,224-mile journey from Quebec City to Vancouver. The 2850 steamed across the country through 25 changes of crew without a single engine failure.

Because of this, the "Royal" designation was given to all C.P. Hudson locomotives from 2820 to 2864. The 2850 went on to be exhibited at the 1939 New York's World Fair.

The 2860, built in 1940 for use in British Columbia, was the first engine built as a "Royal Hudson." From 1940 to 1956 she ran through the canyons and tunnels between Vancouver and Revelstoke, hauling the great transcontinental passenger trains.

But technology finally caught up with the steam locomotives. Diesels replaced them and most of the Royal Hudsons, including the 2860, were retired to the scrap heap and left to rust.

Luckily, though, that was not the fate of 2860. In 1973, the Government of British Columbia purchased the Royal Hudson 2860. She was restored, and on June 20, 1974, began a brand new career.

Today, from mid-May to mid-September, she hauls 11 ex-C.P.R. 1940s coaches, a baggage car and a dining car through some of the most beautiful mountain and ocean scenery in Canada. The 55 kilometre return journey from North Vancouver to Squamish and back takes more than 800 sightseeing passengers along Howe Sound. The train goes over trestles and through the tunnels of the British Columbia Railway line.

It is a journey, for some, of long-ago memories. For children, it is a journey of adventure and excitement. For the Royal Hudson, it is a journey that honours the era of the steam locomotives.

Loading the trains!

7. Vancouver Goes to Work

For a young child like me growing up in Vancouver, our first exposure to work was Mama working around the house every day.

Of course, we were always too busy to notice what she did—sweeping, polishing, dusting—unless she was sewing.

For Mama, sewing was her pride and joy. She made all our clothes, and when she had the time, clothes for herself too. If she were alive today, she would find all kinds of markets for her lace and embroidery work through the craft outlets. But, in Vancouver's early days, the Mamas only sewed for their families.

Mama once made me a beautiful green velvet dress. It was made from the left-over material of a gorgeous dress she made for herself with leg-of-mutton sleeves. How I loved that little dress! Mama had hand-crocheted a snowy white collar that contrasted brilliantly with the rich green of the velvet.

7) I spy with my little eye
a place that's all covered with glass.
But you'd better watch out
'cause the judges might pout
if you're caught being bad
for a farce!

77

Before 1922, motorists drove English-fashion on the left side of the road. In 1922, the law was changed so that people had to drive on the right-hand side of the road.

In 1925, the B.C. Motor Act introduced speed limits on the roads; 40 kilometres in open country and 25 kilometres on city streets and wooded country.

The first motor vehicle to appear in British Columbia was brought in by a Vancouver businessman named William Henry Armstrong. In 1899 he bought a "Stanley Steamer" for $650. It cost him another $350 to ship it from Newton, Massachusetts, where it was made, to Vancouver, and on September 24, he went out for his first drive. In the passenger seat was none other than His Worship, Mayor Garden.

The car looked like a small buggy. It was propelled by steam, had rubber tires, and was fitted with a small bell to warn people of its approach. . . .

Mama made everything for us when we were babies. All in white. There were crocheted bonnets, socks, and dresses. She made booties and shirts for John and Billy and later on, made them their first pants and undershirts.

Mama, of course, made all of her full length skirts and snowy white aprons. Everything was trimmed with crocheted lace, and when she washed them in the tub, they all received a stiff dose of starch to keep them in shape.

Mama's work every day was to fight the dust in the house. There was ALWAYS dust brought in on our boots or blown in from the dirt-track streets. A lot of the dust would gather in the ruching in the bottom of the skirt. No amount of brushing would rid the ruching of all the dust, and often, Mama would rip it off and replace it with new ruching.

You see, back then, there were no vacuum cleaners to get rid of the dirt and there were no dry cleaners or launderettes where you could take your dirty clothes. They'd be hand washed in the tub and one of my earliest images of Mama is the sight of her trim body clad in long sweeping skirts and aprons bending over a tub full of sudsy dirty water, her arms soaked to the elbows. She had her long, dark hair piled high on her head, and ringlets would slip from their hold and stick to her sweating forehead as she worked at getting rid of "the devil dirt."

And, all the time, she would sneeze.

It was a long time before Mama realized she had allergies. She would dust and sneeze and sweep and sneeze and wash and sneeze her way through the day. Day after day. She never had a cold and it never

8) I spy with my little eye
a street with a name
from the past.
Of a man once a Lord
people simply adored
'cause his name was a town
that would last.

A lot of the boys were dressed alike when we were growing up. Do you like Mama's handiwork!?

occurred to us children that there was anything wrong. Sneezing was just Mama's way. Like sewing.

Of course, Mama taught me to sew. But I wanted to do more than just sew when I grew up. And as Mama and Daddy took us to see the sights of Vancouver over the years, I knew that there were so many things you could be!

I can remember when Mama and Daddy took all of us one Saturday afternoon to a fish cannery. What a smell! But I was so fascinated with the assembly line of Indian women cutting fish that I didn't let the smell bother me.

Fish canning had started in Vancouver even before Vancouver was incorporated. A man called James Symes experimented in 1867 with preserving salmon in sealed cans. By the 1890s there were lots of canneries set up on the Fraser River and the coastal areas. Vancouver traded canned salmon with England and Australia, and fish packed in ice was shipped by rail to Eastern Canada and the Eastern United States.

It was exciting, watching all those women handle the slippery fish. Then I thought about all the men in their fishing trawlers in the Strait of Georgia and I decided that

Indian women canning salmon.

the fishing industry must be one of the most exciting places to work in. I decided I was going to be an assembly line fish cutter when I grew up.

That was before the circus came to town. I changed my mind about being a fish cutter when I saw the lovely girls riding bareback on beautiful horses and doing tricks. I wanted to be a bareback rider instead when I grew up.

I must have been very easily influenced when I was growing up because I changed my mind again one night after Daddy had taken me to the theatre.

We were walking past the Vancouver Hotel on the corner of Granville and Georgia Streets. From the street you could look down through the windows into the basement and see the Chinese bakers getting the dough ready. They would bake it at night so that there would be fresh bread to serve in the restaurant the next day.

I couldn't help but stop and watch. There was so much dough that they had to use a pole to knead it. (Kneading dough means mixing all the ingredients together and folding air into it until the dough is firm and elastic.) One of the Chinese bakers actually rode the pole up and down until the dough was properly kneaded!

I was fascinated! I decided right then that I was going to be a dough mixer when I grew up so that I could ride the pole up and down. . . .

We loved the Chinese. Daddy said they were really hard workers and they were always so polite and friendly. They used to make John and me giggle, too. You see, in China, they always walked in line, one behind another. When they came to British Columbia to work on the railroad they still walked that way. When they became merchants in Vancouver, they'd walk in file with their choppy little steps and babble away to each other over their shoulders in Chinese. We hadn't the faintest idea what they were talking about but their voices were so sing-song and their scuttry walk so different, we couldn't help but giggle.

Mama wouldn't let us giggle when they came to the door selling fruits and vegetables. They were so polite. They'd weigh everything out in wicker baskets then bring it all into the kitchen.

At Christmas, our Chinese deliveryman always brought Mama a lovely dish full of narcissus and a piece

A TEST OF FAITH

Could a Chinese man be forced to cut off his pigtail?

NEVER! Most people would have argued at the turn of the century. But one rancher in New Westminster could argue differently.

He had caught a Chinese man stealing chickens from his chicken coop. He tied him to a fence by his pigtail then left him with a cup of water and a knife to decide for himself what he was going to do.

It wouldn't take us long to decide that our only means of escape would be to cut our hair and escape. But it took the Chinese man 24 HOURS to decide to cut off his pigtail.

He must have really suffered, wondering what he was going to tell his friends and relatives when they saw him without his queue...

Publisher's file

Chinese vendor delivering fruits and vegetables to homes.

The symbol of Chinese pigtails

The Chinese men who first worked in Vancouver wore their hair in pigtails. Sometimes, they were called 'queues.' Because they never cut their hair, the pigtails were so long they would tuck them into their pockets or wrap them around their heads under their hats.

The Chinese men had been forced to wear pigtails by the Manchus 300 years ago. In 1644, the Manchus conquered China and established the Ch'ing Dynasty. They forced the Chinese to serve under them. The pigtail was a symbol of their loss of freedom and independence.

Three hundred years is a long time and gradually they thought it was an honour to wear pigtails. In fact, imprisoned Chinese men in Vancouver were excused from having their hair cut by prison barbers because of the humiliation they would suffer.

In China, the Chinese became more and more rebellious against the Manchu government. The Manchu officials tried to reform their laws. But, in 1911, a rebellion broke out and, in February, 1912, the Manchu government collapsed.

As a symbol of their regained freedom after 300 years of servitude, the Chinese cut off their pigtails.

of ginger. I think everyone got some ginger.

The Chinese worked as houseboys, too, for the wealthy. I used to wonder what it would be like to have a houseboy but Daddy never made enough money as a carpenter for me to find out.

There were lots of home deliveries in the early days of Vancouver. Things like fruits, vegetables, milk, bread, fish, and coal. We didn't have freezers then so, in the summer, merchants would deliver ice. They'd bring it right to the door and put it in the icebox for you. In the early 1900s it was about 1¢ for one pound of ice. The ice came in blocks. I remember, when the deliveryman was inside delivering the ice, the children would steal the icechips and suck on them.

There were some deliverymen I hated, though. They were the beer wagon drivers who would take the barrels of beer from the breweries to the liquor stores.

Granville Street between 7th and 9th Avenues was steep and I'll never forget, one winter day, watching a team of horses trying to pull a heavy beer wagon up the icy slope.

The low-slung wagon was loaded with great big heavy barrels. The driver sat way up high with a whip and he was whipping and slashing the horses who were frantically slipping on the ice. They'd fall right to their knees and cut them and the blood would be pouring

THE SILK TRAIN EXPRESS LEFT ROYALTY WAITING

Long ago and far away, the wife of a Chinese Emperor, Huang Ti, made a discovery that would change the world of trade and commerce.

In 2640 B.C., the Empress discovered that the filament from the caterpillar of a moth species could be twisted and woven into a lustrous fabric that came to be known as silk. Very soon, she had clothed herself and her Court in the most beautiful silken garments the world had ever seen. Silk became the most prized of fabrics.

It was just as valuable in the early 1900s when it was in demand by New York fashion designers. As a result, shipments of silk from the Orient to New York via the Port of Vancouver were given the utmost priority.

Both raw (cocoons with live silkworms inside) and manufactured silk were shipped. When a ship was coming in from Shanghai, Hong Kong, Canton, Kobe, or Yokohama, telegrams would alert the crews in Vancouver. A train would be made, steamed up and waiting on the track for the silk boat to dock. Each silk train would have about a dozen cars and each car could hold 470 bales of silk.

The moment the ship was tied up, conveyors would be run right into the silk rooms on board. A steady stream of silk bales would be conveyed onto the train. Last to be loaded would be the cocoons which would be put in a car of their own.

The entire business of simultaneously loading the cars would be done in less than 8 minutes. The paper work would be completed, and within 20 minutes, the train would be rolling.

Nothing stopped a silk train. Not a signal. Not a stoplight. With so much at stake—sometimes a shipment would be worth more than $10 million, a fortune in those days—a railman risked instant dismissal if he delayed the shipment for a moment.

Even the Royal Specials—the trains carrying British Royalty—had to wait for the silk trains. Once, when the Duke of York, later King George VI, was en route from Hong Kong to London via Canada, the Royal Special was shunted to a siding. When he asked why, he was told, "We had to let a silk train go by. In Canada, silk has rights over everything."

One day, though, something terrible happened. Not far from Yale in the Fraser Valley, a silk train was speeding around a corner when the fifth car from the engine jumped the track and plunged into the river taking with it all the cars behind. The cars broke and out floated all the bales of silk.

It was a million dollar wreck. Some of the silk was lost forever. Some was rescued by Indians who were paid a reward of $5 a bale. Some ended up in private homes as souvenirs.

In one home, some of the silk was used to stuff a homemade quilt.

Years later, the quilt was given away to a rummage sale. Years after that, the new owner of the quilt took it to a woollen outlet to have it repaired. Imagine her surprise when she learned that it had not been stuffed with wool but with pure, raw silk!

By the sheer stroke of fate, a friend of a friend of hers was none other than the lady who had given the quilt to the rummage sale. Today, so the story goes, the quilt is living out its life on a houseboat on the Fraser River where it almost perished at the beginning of the century.

The era of the silk trains continued until 1939 when the last of the silk trains was taken out of service. In 1942, all C.P.R. silk cars were demoted to ordinary freight cars and the excitement of silk runs was gone forever.

The cultivation of silk

The cultivation of silk is called "sericulture." This means, the care of the domestic silkworm from egg stage to the completion of the cocoon. Sericulture includes the cultivation of mulberry trees because silkworms feed on the mulberry leaves.

During the feeding stage, the worm (or larvae) goes through 4 stages of growth. At the end of each stage, it sheds its skin. After it has shed its fourth skin, at about 6-8 weeks of life, it is ready to begin spinning its cocoon.

In silk culture, the worms are placed in racks containing small cells. Here the worms spin their cocoons over a period of 4-5 days.

This is the time when they actually make or "spin" the silk. Inside the body of each silkworm are 2 silk glands which secrete a liquid through a single exit tube in the worm's head called a "spinneret."

The liquid hardens in the air and forms 2 filaments, or strands. A second pair of glands gives out a gummy substance called sericin which cements the 2 filaments together to form a glossy thread.

A perfect cocoon contains about 1,000 metres of silk. Twelve kilograms of cocoons yields one kilogram of raw silk. During the making of silk fabric, sericin is left on the fibre until the fabric has been woven. It is then washed in soap and water so that the sericin is dissolved away, leaving the silk with its characteristic lustrous and soft feel.

THE PORT OF VANCOUVER
Highlights of 100 Years

- **1864** *Ellen Lewis* sailed on November 9 with 150,000 metres of lumber and 16,000 for Australia. The first export from Burrard Inlet.
- **1875** Point Atkinson lighthouse started operation.
- **1883** On March 15 *Duke of Abercorn* arrived in Port Moody with the first shipment of steel for C.P.R. construction.
- **1884** The C.P.R. terminus was changed from Port Moody to Vancouver.
- **1890** C.P.R. Pier "A" constructed.
- **1891** The first of the C.P.R.-owned Empress liners, *Empress of India*, went into service on the Oriental run. Union Steamships Pier was built and the harbour offices were constructed.
- **1893** Canadian-Australian line established.
- **1895** First cargo of wheat sent from B.C.
- **1912** Shipping Federation of B.C. created. Corporation of the Harbour Commission of Vancouver established,
- **1915** LaPointe Pier opened.
- **1923** Ballantyne Pier built.
- **1924** Terminal grain elevator built.
- **1925** Second Narrows Bridge built.
- **1927** Piers "B" and "C" and the Alberta Wheat Pool Elevator dock built.
- **1931** Fisherman's Wharf built.
- **1932** Burrard Bridge built over False Creek.
- **1939** Lions Gate Bridge officially opened by H. M. King George VI.
- **1942** June 20, a Japanese submarine shelled Estevan Point lighthouse.
- **1958** During construction of the new Second Narrows Bridge, the bridge collapsed sending 18 men to their deaths. A rescue diver drowned trying to save the men.
- **1959** The new Second Narrows Bridge completed and Centennial Pier built.
- **1960** Vancouver Wharves built.
- **1964** Port of Vancouver celebrated the centennial of the first export from Burrard Inlet by sponsoring the International Maritime Festival.

9) I spy with my little eye
   hills made of scaffold
   and steel
   where people will queue
   for a turn to turn blue
   as they whizz down the slopes
   with a scream!

Publisher's file

Parents sometimes gave their children a nickel (5¢) to take empty orange boxes and collect horse droppings on the road. The droppings would be used to fertilize the garden. Lots of dads believed the droppings made the roses bloom!

down their legs while the driver kept on whipping their backs. It was HORRIBLE!

"Stop that!" I yelled before Mama could hold me back.

"Be off with ya, girl!" he shouted at me.

"You're making the horses BLEED!" I yelled again.

"Be quiet, Mary-Margaret," Mama said sternly but I didn't listen.

"You're nothing but a wicked...cruel...."

That was when Mama grabbed me by my shoulder and pushed me in another direction. I was so angry at the driver, nothing she could say would make me feel sorry for shouting at the driver.

A few weeks later, something happened to Billy to make Mama change her mind about beer wagon drivers.

Only that week, we had celebrated Billy's 6th birthday. On Friday, he came running into our house crying his eyes out. Mama and I rushed to see what was the matter. As soon as I saw him, I stopped, horrified. His head was bleeding and the back of his shirt was torn and his back was bleeding from a gash, too.

"Billy, what HAPPENED?" Mama asked him as she rushed him to the bathroom to strip him down and wash him.

At first, he sobbed so much he couldn't answer. By this time, Daddy, who had just come home from work, joined Mama in the bathroom and together they calmed Billy down.

I cried too when I heard what had happened to him. He had been walking on Granville Street right where we had seen the bleeding horses a few weeks before. He'd found a whip just as a beer wagon was coming up the hill. The driver had stopped the horses and asked him what he had.

"A whip," Billy told him.

"I'll pay you for it if you give it to me," the driver said.

Billy handed him the whip but, instead of getting some money for it, the driver lifted it up and whipped him! It slashed right across his back. Then the man whipped the horses and drove away, laughing!

Daddy was FURIOUS. Mama cried with anger and hurt, too. Billy and I never forgot the cruelty of those drivers. Daddy tried to find out who had whipped him

Everyone—children, cats, and dogs—welcomed the delivery of ice in summer!

but no one among the wagon drivers was telling so we never did find out.

As we grew older, we found out that not all the drivers were cruel like that. Many were kind to their horses and took special care of them in the winter when the roads were dangerous.

By this time, in the early 1900s, all kinds of industries were growing in Vancouver. The most important ones were those that developed by selling the natural things that could be found in the province: lumber, fish, minerals, metals, and, later, hydro power. All these things are B.C.'s natural resources.

Of course, in a way, the lumber industry had started when the Spanish settled at Nootka Sound in 1789 and built a fort from local timber.

Lumber was first exported from Burrard Inlet in 1864, and by 1900, huge amounts were being shipped to Australia, South Africa, South America, the United Kingdom, and China. More and more sawmills were built to keep up with the demand for B.C. lumber.

I think it's sad when a tragedy in one part of the world brings work and profits to another part.

Like the San Francisco earthquake.

On April 18, 1906, a terrible earthquake destroyed San Francisco. It started a horrible fire that destroyed the centre of the town and burned for 3 days before the

Deas (Massey) Island tunnel opened in 1959.

In 1911, married women were given the right to vote.

Publisher's file

In 1858, gold was discovered along the banks of the Fraser River. The discovery started a gold rush which brought many prospectors and settlers to the region.

rains put it out. Seven hundred people died, 250,000 were homeless, and 512 city blocks were in ruins.

To rebuild the city, the construction industry bought great quantities of B.C. fir lumber, twice as much as it usually bought through Vancouver.

When an earthquake hit Valparaiso in Chile in August, 1906, (the same year as the San Francisco earthquake) another flood of orders came in. I suppose the business was really good for the forestry industry here but what a lot of sadness there must have been in those other places.

A few years after the year of the earthquakes, a huge cargo of lumber was shipped to the Panama for the construction of the famous canal.

In 1911, the forestry industry developed newsprint for newspapers, and newsprint mills and pulp mills began to appear. Sawmilling and pulp and paper became such huge industries, that for many decades, they were the most important in the province.

Mining was also important. In fact, it was mining— the search for gold— that opened up British Columbia even more than forestry. Mining camps encouraged people to settle nearby and that led to the creation of roads and towns.

In the late 1800s, silver-lead ore was discovered in the Kootenays. Then, after the Second World War, a major mining expansion happened when Japan imported iron ore, copper, and coal from this province.

Of course, all these metals were used in industries in Vancouver and other cities in Canada, too. Copper was needed for the thousands of miles of telegraph wires that were put up across the country. The overhead electric lines for the tramways and railways created heavy demands for copper, lead, and zinc.

During the World Wars, there were "war industries"— industries that made the tools, ammunition, transportation, and supplies for wartime.

I wasn't very old when I first learned that people's feelings toward each other change between what Daddy calls the "good years," when there's lots of jobs, and the "bad years," when jobs are rare.

"Those Orientals are going to have to go back to their own country," Daddy was saying to Mama in a

The loggers used the meanest looking saws I have ever seen to cut the trees!

Oxen (above)...horses...and trains (below)...they were all used to haul timber from the forest to the mills.

Logging was one of the first industries in the area that would become Vancouver. In 1863, Pioneer Mills began operation on the north shore of Burrard Inlet. It shipped lumber to New Westminster, Victoria, and Nanaimo. On November 9, 1864, the sailing ship, *Ellen Lewis* left the inlet for Australia with a cargo of lumber. It was the first export shipment of goods from what would be Vancouver.

In 1867, the famous Hastings Mill opened on the south shore of the inlet. It was operated by Captain Edward Stamp. The mill's steampowered saws cut about 9,230 metres of lumber a day. The timber was hauled to the mill by teams of oxen.

The Royal City Planing Mill on False Creek was still being built when the Great Fire broke out in 1886. Victims of the fire were brought here before being buried.

Mill Lumber Carrier, 1925.

One of the most important entrepreneurs and businessmen in the 1860s was Captain Edward Stamp. In 1861, he established the first important mill on Vancouver Island.

As a shipmaster, he knew the value of good timber for masts and spars. When he first saw the coastal forests of Douglas fir and cedar, he was very impressed. He was SO impressed with the wood that he arranged with the British government to send them a 46 metre flagpole to be put up in London's famous Kew Gardens. By 1861, a Douglas fir flagpole had been installed and it stood in Kew for 50 years.

One of the largest cedars stood in North Vancouver. In the 1890s it was recorded as being 6 metres in diameter at ground level.

voice that sounded as though he was really mad at something.

I peaked through the crack in the kitchen door. Billy had shoved a toy through the door last week and Daddy didn't have enough money to fix the hole. I frowned, wondering why he wanted the Chinese to go home. He'd always LOVED them!

"Do you really think so?" Mama asked him. "After all, they did help to build the railway."

"That's not the point!" Daddy argued. "If there's enough work, it's OK for them to be in Vancouver. But if there's not. . .we jus' don't need them here, that's all!"

Later, I asked Mama why he felt that way.

"People are fighting for jobs these days, Mary-Margaret," Mama said, "Daddy's just. . .frustrated."

"With the Chinese?"

"With everything," Mama sighed and looked at me. "There are all kinds of people in Canada. They all helped to build it one way or another. But, when things get bad and jobs are scarce, they all think they deserve the jobs more than the other. . ."

What Mama was talking about, of course, was prejudice. Racial prejudice. The white people thought they were better than the Chinese and the East Indians. They thought they deserved first chance at any job. They clashed over jobs in the hard years (1904 and 1907) when businesses weren't able to sell their products and there were few jobs.

John never had any trouble getting his first job. He knew, from the very first time he laid eyes on an Empress liner, exactly what he wanted to be. A bridge messenger!

Of course, he wasn't any different from any other boy. They ALL wanted to be bridge messengers, sail on

A Japanese family.

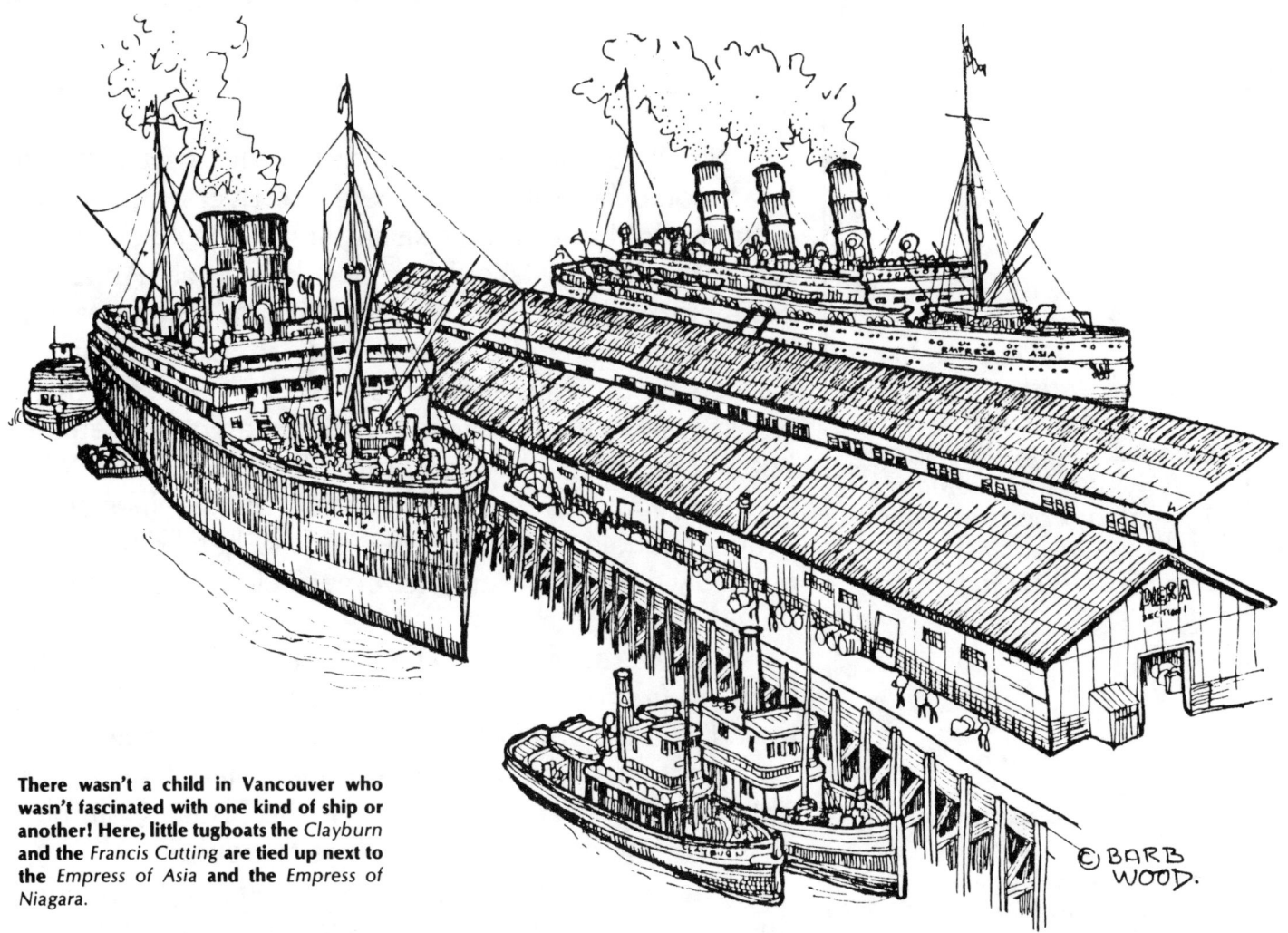

There wasn't a child in Vancouver who wasn't fascinated with one kind of ship or another! Here, little tugboats the *Clayburn* and the *Francis Cutting* are tied up next to the *Empress of Asia* and the *Empress of Niagara*.

the Empress ships, and have adventures in the Orient.

A bridge messenger is a boy who stands watch on the bridge and is at the instant beck and call to run messages. The boys wear navy-type bell-bottomed trousers and a cap with the ship's name on it. Each ship carries 3 messengers, one for each watch.

John joined the Sea Cadet Corps of the Navy League of Canada and he was recruited from there. We all went down to the wharf on the day he sailed on the *Empress of India*. He was so proud and excited! So was Daddy. Mama cried, Billy wailed, and I wished that girls could work on ships, too.

Because Vancouver is a port city, there was all kinds of work connected with the water. Like tugboating.

The first tugboat on the Pacific Coast was really a steamboat. In 1825, the Hudson's Bay Company set up its headquarters at Fort Vancouver on the Columbia River. In 1826, George Simpson was made governor-in-chief and one of his first problems was to solve the difficulties the Hudson's Bay's trading ships had navigating the coastal waters.

More than 2,300 vessels flying the flags of more than 50 countries use the Port of Vancouver facilities every year. With more than 50 berths, the port ranks second in North America and is the busiest on the Pacific coast.

Each year, about 160,000 cruise passengers visit our city, docking at the Port of Vancouver.

At first, the area we know of as British Columbia was called New Caledonia. In 1858, the British Government renamed New Caledonia and called it the Colony of British Columbia. The colony consisted only of the mainland with Fort Langley as its capital.

The first Europeans to come to British Columbia's coast came in search of a Northwest Passage. Explorers had been looking for a northern route to the Orient ever since England's King Henry VII had sent John Cabot in search of unknown lands to develop trade and return merchandise to England. In 1497, Cabot searched for a western route to the Orient but he was not successful. The Europeans traded with the Orientals for silks and spices. They believed that, if a sea route in a northwest direction could be found, it would shorten the travelling time between the Orient and Europe, speed up trade, and increase profits.

Mr. Simpson came up with the idea that a steamboat would be able to navigate the rivers, inlets, and sounds a lot better than a sailing ship. They'd be able to reach trading posts quicker and beat their American competitors by taking on furs, fish, and timber faster. The goods could be transferred from steamboat to sailing ship quickly for shipment to China and Europe.

It was 10 years before Mr. Simpson got his steamboat. *The Beaver* arrived on the Pacific coast in 1836. She was about 33 metres long and had 2 engines which drove a paddle wheel on either side of her. The boilers burned wood or coal and her crew included more than a dozen woodcutters.

She was supposed to be a freighter, but, right from her very first day of operation, May 17, 1836, when she towed *The Columbia* to a sawmill, she was a towboat.

Since then, towboats, or tugboats, have been a daily sight on the waters up and down the British Columbia coast, towing everything from logs to houses.

The early years of the 1920s were good years. Business grew and the city expanded. Radio broadcasting began in 1922. The Second Narrows Bridge was built and the new campus of the University of British Columbia opened at Point Grey in October, 1925.

But everything stopped in 1929 when the Great Depression started. Life was hard for everyone for the next 6 years. In fact, by the end of 1935, Vancouver was almost totally broke.

But not quite. Business had begun to pick up in 1934. A new city hall was finished in 1936. Lions Gate Bridge was built in 1938. In 1939, the new Hotel Vancouver was built on the corner of Georgia and Burrard Streets. King George VI and Queen Elizabeth visited Vancouver, and war broke out in Europe again.

Nothing much changed in Vancouver until December, 1941, when Japan bombed Pearl Harbor in Hawaii. There was instant panic and Vancouver was plunged into an immediate "black-out." What happened was that every light in the city was turned off. People put up black drapes across their windows and the city was hidden in total darkness.

It was frightening. We were afraid the Japanese would bomb our city. But they never did. The

An early steamboat at work.

Americans retaliated by dropping an atom bomb on Hiroshima and Nagasaki.

When major events are going on, like a World War, it's funny how you remember the little things.

Like stockings.

Mama always wore silk stockings. How I loved the fine, soft feel of them! But, because of the war, no silk was brought in from the Orient. Manufacturers began making nylon stockings but Mama and all her friends hated them.

"They don't fit properly, Mary-Margaret," she said.

"So you're going to PAINT your legs instead?" I asked her incredulously.

She looked sort of defensive, "So's everyone else."

"Everyone else" meant all the women Mama worked with at the department store. I watched as she glossed brown stain over her legs then, with a fine brush, painted a black "seam" line up the back. (All stockings had a seam line then, from the heel to the top of the thigh. Well-dressed women made sure the seam line was always straight.)

I looked outside. Heavy clouds were piling up and, already, drops of rain were splattering on the window. I stared at Mama's legs again, beautifully painted to look like she was wearing real stockings, then I looked out of the window again.

"Think you can make it to work in time?" I grinned.

Mama scowled, grabbed her coat and ran out of the door. But she didn't make it in time. She told me later, that by the time she got to work, the rain had washed her

Golden Prairie nugget

The first shipment of prairie grain through the Port of Vancouver was 2,000 tonnes of wheat consigned to Europe on the U.S. steamer *Effingham*. It sailed on January 7, 1921, with wheat purchased from the Alberta Pacific Grain Co. Ltd.

Today, 5 working elevators now process nearly 11 million tonnes of grain each year. Ten bulk cargo vessels can load grain at any one time. It would take 345 ships each handling 30,000 tonnes to move the annual grain shipment from Vancouver.

The grain arrives by the dock in train hopper cars. Each car carries from 80 to 90 tonnes of grain.

Between 550 and 650 hopper cars can pour their grain into the elevators in 24 hours. Once inside, the grain is cleaned and graded then loaded onto waiting ships. Over 20,000 tonnes of grain may be loaded in a single day.

The Port of Vancouver now handles over 40 percent of all exported Canadian grain.

Captain Cook and his companions were the first Europeans to set foot on British Columbia soil. They came ashore at Nootka Sound in 1778. They traded iron, copper, and other trinkets for silky smooth sea-otter skins offered by the Indians.

Captain Cook's ships, HMS *Resolution* and HMS *Discovery* in Nootka Sound, 1778.

Airways not for the birds

The Pacific coast has always been a major flyway for migrating birds and home for huge flocks of shore birds like dunlins and sandpipers. They lived along shores; and on the grass near the runways. They would fly in great flocks around the runways just as planes were taking off.

In an incident in the 1960s, a flock of dunlins hit a plane during takeoff. The flock did $150,000 damage to the engines and 2,000 birds were killed.

Because birds are a constant hazard to the safety of planes, special efforts are taken to keep the runways clear of birds. They are scared away with the use of loud noises, lights, and tapes of squawking birds.

Today, Vancouver International Airport is recognized as a world leader in bird control. It was one of the first to pioneer the idea of using trained falcons to scare away seagulls. The airport receives letters from airports all around the world asking about the most successful methods of dealing with the hazards of birds.

"stockings" away and she had felt as barelegged as a baby!

We never let her forget the day she painted her clothes on. . . .

The war ended in 1945, and from then on, Vancouver grew quickly. The first television program reached the city from Seattle in 1948 and the first chair lift was built on Grouse Mountain in 1949.

The 1950s were great years of expansion. By now, the city had grown so much that many people lived in the suburbs. Roads, tunnels, bridges, and highways made travel from the suburbs to the city fast. Businesses moved from the city to the suburbs and the vacant areas were remodelled for housing, marinas, walkways, and parks. The City of Vancouver became more and more beautiful.

It was a special day when a statue of "Gassy Jack" Deighton was put up in Maple Tree Square in 1970. It was as though Vancouver had stopped what it was doing to remember its beginning.

The sun sparkled on the brand new statue. The sparkles made me think, that was how he had been when he had first come to Granville nearly 100 years ago. John Deighton had been a sparkle of spirit and hope and energy. He had believed that great things would happen to Vancouver.

Vancouver City Archives.

The *Santa Saturnina* casts anchor at Point Grey, 1791.

The first European to see the future site of the City of Vancouver was Lieutenant Jose Maria Narvaez in the **Santa Saturnina.** *It was he who charted the coastline around Boundary Bay and Point Roberts.*
Narvaez was the first European to make contact with the mainland Indians. He traded sheets of copper and pieces of iron for meat, vegetables, water, and firewood.

And they have.

Vancouver today has all kinds of businesses and industries, arts, and crafts to offer the world. People come here from all over to trade and enjoy our products and services and gasp at the beauty of our home by the river, sea, and mountains.

It's fun, growing up. It's challenging, too. And sometimes it's hard. Because things change and you have to learn to change with them. The two World Wars, the Great Depression, and the difficult times in between, all had an effect on Vancouver. But people got over the hard times by looking forward to the good times ahead.

And, now, the good times are here. Vancouver is an international city with sisters all around the world. She is beautiful and famous, cultured, and talented. But, more than that, she has a special feeling of warmth, love, and energy about her that makes people want to be here.

If Vancouver were a real person, Mama and Daddy would say, "She's maturing."

Which means, *You're All Grown Up, Vancouver!*

10) I spy with my little eye
a bay where the waves meet the land;
and the town celebrates
its seawater fate
as children carve dreams
in the sand.

Vancouver International Airport

It cost 25¢ to be admitted to one of the most spectacular events of the Great Depression years.

It was July 22, 1932. Everyone was going to the Air Pageant. It was the day of the official opening of Vancouver's International Airport.

There was formation flying by the Royal Canadian Air Force "Silver Siskins;" 'crazy flying' by airmail pilot Captain Bernard Martin; upside-down flying by Captain Jack Sanderson and the Transport Ship Display in which 4 planes demonstrated the speed, comfort, and stability of modern aircraft.

An air service had already been established on Lulu Island before the opening of Vancouver International Airport. B. B. Airways had been running a flight between Vancouver and Victoria since 1928. The Lulu Island site was not adequate enough for a growing airport and the Sea Island site was thought to be the best in the province.

Air transport was not taken seriously at first. The entire crew at the airport consisted of 3 men, a horse, and a homemade wagon. The horse was bought for $35 complete with harness. It was the most economical thing the airport ever had. It could feed on airport grass and produce its own fertilizer at the same time.

The airport didn't have much business at first.

"We had no night lighting, no traffic control, no weather bureau, and no radio aids," said Bill Templeton who was the airport's first manager.

A pilot called Joe Bertalino remembers a saying they used to use to report the weather on a radio to Seattle: "If you can see Mount Baker, it's going to rain. If you can't see it, it IS raining."

The 1930s were the years of barnstorming. That was when people paid to go on sightseeing flights over the city or the country.

The first organized group to rent space at the airport was the Aero Club of B.C. Then, in 1934, United Air Lines began a trial service between Vancouver and Seattle. Vancouver became the first foreign port to be served by United.

Canadian Airways started a rival service. On its first flight to Seattle, its plane, a Lockheed 10A, carried Mayor Gerry McGeer and his entire council. They flew to Seattle for lunch and came back to Vancouver in time for a 2:00 p.m. meeting. The lunch flight was supposed to show Vancouver businessmen the speed and convenience of air transport!

The airport grew in the years ahead. It was made available to the Armed Forces during the Second World War.

After the war, the airport got even busier. The jet age arrived. Planes were landing and taking off every few minutes.

Captain George Vancouver.

The Story of Captain George Vancouver

HMS *Discovery* with HMS *Chatham* in background. These were Captain Vancouver's ships as he left Falmouth, England, 1491.

Captain George Vancouver was born on June 22, 1757, in King's Lynn, Norfolk, England.

At the age of 13, he entered the navy and accompanied Captain James Cook on his second (1772-1775) voyage and his third (1776-1780) voyage.

The story of Captain Vancouver's own expedition to the Pacific Northwest is a story of European politics.

In the late 1700s, many exlorers, hunters, and merchants were flocking to the west coast of North America in search of furs. The traders were English, Spanish, and American and they competed heavily among each other for fur pelts.

The Spanish were very protective of their trading rights. In 1789, they built a fort at Nootka Sound. A man called Martinez took charge of it and arrested 4 British trading ships owned by Captain John Meares.

Captain Meares was very angry at having his ships taken away. He asked the British Government to do something about it, and in 1790, a big argument began between Britain and Spain.

The Spanish claimed the right of ownership of the whole northwest coast of America. The British argued that they could only possess the land they actually occupied.

The British got so angry they threatened to go to war over the problem. The Spanish government backed down. On October 28, 1790, Spain and Britain signed the Nootka Convention agreeing that each nation was free to sail and fish in the Pacific and trade and set up settlements on unoccupied land. Spain also agreed to give to Britain the property at Nootka Sound.

By now, George Vancouver was a captain in charge of his own fleet. He was asked to return to the Pacific Northwest and take possession of the land and buildings at Nootka Sound. He was also instructed to chart the coastline and find out if a Northwest Passage existed.

Captain Vancouver sailed from Falmouth, England, in HMS *Discovery*. The second ship in his expedition was called HMS *Chatham*. "HMS" stands for His (or Her) Majesty's Service.

The expedition sailed on April 1, 1791. Vancouver sailed for the Cape of Good Hope at the southern tip of South Africa. Then he sailed for Australia and the Pacific Ocean. He arrived off the British Columbia coast in the spring of 1792.

In the yawl of the *Discovery*, Vancouver charted Point Grey. He entered the inlet which he named Burrard's Canal after his friend, Sir Harry Burrard. Then he followed First Narrows.

"We were met by about 50 Indians in their canoes," he wrote in his journal on June 13, 1792, "who conducted themselves with great decorum and civility, presenting us with several fish cooked.... These good people, finding we were inclined to make some return for their hospitality, showed much understanding in preferring iron to copper...."

He wrote about the scenery, too.

"The shores...on the southern side...though rocky are well covered with trees of a large growth, particularly the pine tribe. On the northern side, the rugged, snowy barrier...was only protected from the wash of the sea by a very narrow border of low land."

Captain Vancouver went on to explore the coastline some more and named Puget Sound and the Strait of Georgia. In August, he met with the Spaniards to take over their settlement at Nootka Sound.

He continued to survey the west coast from California to Alaska during 1793, and in 1794, returned home to England. He died 4 years later on May 10, 1798, in Richmond, Surrey, England, at the age of 40 years.

More books to read

The Pacific Coast	Fred Bodsworth
The Vancouver Guide Book	Ginny & Beth Evans
Lower Fraser Valley, Evolution of a Cultural Landscape	Alfred H. Siemens, Editor
Vancouver's First Century, A City Album	Edited by: N. Kloppenborg Alice Niwinski Eve Johnson with Robert Gruetter
Vancouver's Past	Raymond Hull Gordon Soules Christine Soules
Vancouver	Eric Nicol
Against Wind and Weather	Ken Druska
British Columbia Disasters	Derek Pethick
Stanley Park Explorer	Richard M. Steele
It Began with a Ronald	Alex Matches
The Patricks	Eric Whitehead

I SPY ANSWERS

1) **Canadian National Station on Main Street**
2) **The whales at the Vancouver Aquarium**
3) **The Miniature Railway at the Children's Zoo**
4) **The Planetarium**
5) **Maple Tree Square with statue of Gassy Jack Deighton**
6) **Kids' Only Market at Granville Island**
7) **Court House**
8) **Granville Street**
9) **The roller-coaster at Playland**
10) **English Bay (where the Sea Festival is celebrated)**

QUIZ — Z — Z — Z

Test your recall skills, and your research skills. These questions are for your fun - you find the answers.

1) Who was known as the "Godfather of Vancouver?"
2) Who came to Vancouver with a keg of whiskey?
3) Who was the first explorer to see the site where Vancouver would one day be located?
4) Who were "The Three Greenhorns?"
5) What was Vancouver's name before it was called Vancouver?
6) What was the first thing the city council bought after the Great Fire of 1886?
7) Who was Stanley Park named after?
8) What are the names of the 3 whales in the Vancouver Aquarium?
9) What was the number of the C.P.R.'s first engine to arrive in Vancouver in 1887?
10) What important commodity was shipped from the Orient to Vancouver in the first few decades of the 20th century?
11) When was the School Act passed?
12) When did UBC move to its current location at Point Grey?
13) What is the "Knights of Pythias?"
14) Who was "Black Joe?"
15) When was the first Vancouver Symphony Orchestra formed?
16) What was the name of the movie shown on the opening night of The Orpheum?
17) What was the first animal kept on display at Stanley Park?
18) When was the Great Depression?
19) What was known as "a jungle?"
20) Who was Vancouver's first police chief?
21) Who were the first 3 dogs in Vancouver's dog squad?
22) When did Vancouver buy its first fireboat?
23) What was the name of the family who brought ice hockey to Vancouver.
24) When did the B.C. Lions win the Grey Cup?
25) What were Vancouver's first 2 industries?
26) What "island" isn't an island at all?
27) How many "sisters" does Vancouver have?
28) What is Vancouver International Airport famous for among other airports around the world?
29) What terrifying epidemic killed hundreds of Indians in the 1860s.
30) What was the most important train on the C.P.R. track in the early 1900s.
31) What was the tallest tree in Vancouver?